AF696809

FLEMING'S FUNDAMENTALS OF LAW

ESSAY EXAMINATION WRITING WORKBOOK
Volume 1

by

Jeff Alan Fleming
Attorney at Law

Susan Patricia Sneidmiller
Attorney at Law

LEARN TO WRITE . . . THE RIGHT WAY®

Published by: Fleming's Fundamentals of Law
26170 Enterprise Way, Suite 500, Lake Forest, CA 92630
(949) 770-7030 ◆ (800) LAW EXAM
FAX (949) 454-8556 ◆ WEB www.ffol.com
E-MAIL info@ffol.com

Distributed by: Legal Books Distributing
4247 Whiteside Street
Los Angeles, CA 90063
(800) 200-7112

MANAGING WRITER AND EDITOR

Susan Patricia Sneidmiller
Attorney at Law

SUPERVISING WRITER AND EDITOR

Jeff Alan Fleming
Attorney at Law

LAYOUT:

Donald Bayley II
IMAGEN Company Irvine, CA.

SUMMARY OF CONTENTS

SECTION **PAGE**

I. General Considerations 1

II. Skills Tested 1
A. Analysis 1
B. Organization 2
C. Writing 3

III. Recommended Use Of Essay Examination Writing Workbook 4

IV. Preparing For Law School Examinations 5

V. Torts 7

Question #1 Masons v. Finance Co. 9
(Respondeat Superior, Intentional Torts, Damages)

Question #2 Bess v. Jim 25
(Negligence, Negligent Infliction of Emotional Distress)

Question #3 Ace Auto Rental 41
(Vicarious Liability, Negligence, Defenses)

Question #4 Gloria v. Tintco/Mag 57
(Products Liability, Express Warranty, Negligent Misrepresentation, Negligence)

Question #5 Jill v. Don 73
(Intentional Torts, Defamation, Invasion Privacy, Privileges, Business Torts)

VI. Contracts-U.C.C. 87

Question #1 Yellowhouse/Greenhouse 89
(Formation)

Question #2 Motors v. Jones 101
(U.C.C. Formation, Defenses, Damages)

Question #3 Brown v. Mountain Pines 117
(Formation, Tort Crossover)

Question #4 Freeco 133
(U.C.C., Formation, Third Party Beneficiary)

Question #5 Fargo v. Tom 149
(Assignment and Delegation, Conditions and Damages)

VII. Criminal Law 163

Question #1 State v. Dan 165
(Entrapment, Conspiracy, Homicide)

Question #2 State v. Dave 179
(Robbery, Homicide, Defenses)

Question #3 State v. Don/Oscar 193
(Burglary, Homicide, Conspiracy)

Question #4 State v. Bob/Jim 207
(Burglary, Larceny, Homicide, Defenses)

Question #5 State v. Donald 221
(Burglary, Homicide)

FLEMING'S FUNDAMENTALS OF LAW
ESSAY EXAMINATION WRITING WORKBOOK

LEGAL MAXIM

**"Out of the Facts, the Issue Arises
Without Facts, There is no Issue"**

I. GENERAL CONSIDERATIONS

The basic fundamentals of legal writing can be summarized in a simple statement: Legal writing is the process of applying the individual elements from the specific rules of law to specific factual situations upon which justifiable and well organized conclusions are based.

The ability to communicate clearly and concisely in the above manner must be learned and perfected. The earlier you learn the process, the more manageable your study of the law will become. The foundation upon which the technique of legal writing is built involves three distinct skills, which are learned individually and then integrated with practice. The purpose of this book is to identify and demonstrate the skills that you must master as the prerequisite to producing an effective passing essay examination.

II. SKILLS TESTED

A. Analysis

Most law school examinations are presented in the form of factual situations referred to as hypotheticals. The Essay Examination Writing Workbook deals solely with this form of testing.

Analysis is the ability to recognize the facts from the hypothetical that raise the legal issues and to then apply the elements from the applicable rule of law to those issues.

You must be able to read and comprehend the facts as they are given. You will soon realize that it is the facts given in the hypothetical that raise the legal issues. Because of this, you must never underestimate the importance of reading and comprehending the facts. "Fact Sensitivity" is the basis of sound legal reasoning.
The recommended steps that you should follow in sequence for proper legal analysis are:

1. Review the call of the question located at the end of the hypothetical before reading the hypothetical facts. This will help orient your thinking process to the area of law being tested. The call will often narrow the issues and parties that you are to address.

2. Read the hypothetical at least twice from a factual perspective to understand and comprehend the facts.

3. Read the hypothetical for a third time from a legal perspective at which point you may begin analyzing and issue spotting. Remember, the issue arises from the facts.

There are numerous methods that you may utilize to improve your issue spotting. You should seriously consider the following suggestions that will assist you in this area:

1. Develop approaches and issue checklists for each subject. Use the table of contents in your casebook, your class syllabus and/or the table of contents in a commercial outline as your source for development of this tool.

2. Analyze every hypothetical paying special attention to adjectives and adverbs, which are descriptive words, and verbs which are action words. These types of facts are generally issues. Dates and times should never be ignored for the same reason.

3. Analyze each sentence of each paragraph in every hypothetical. Rarely, if ever, does a hypothetical contain totally irrelevant facts. With practice, you will learn to distinguish background facts from issue facts.

4. Analyze every issue by role playing each party's position. This will help you identify counter-arguments to the issues that demand extended analysis.

5. Review and write multiple examinations for each subject area in which you will be tested before sitting for your examination.

Begin the analysis of every hypothetical by allocating approximately 5-7 minutes to the steps suggested in this section.

B. <u>Organization</u>

It is essential for you to be able to organize your issues and arguments in a logical sequence. The student who sees every issue, but is unorganized when presenting the discussion of these issues, will not pass the examination.

The call of the question will often specify the order in which the issues/parties are to be organized. If so, never deviate from the call unless absolutely necessary.

When the call of the question is very general and does not specify the order in which the issues are to be presented, (i.e., Discuss) you may organize according to:

1. The issues that each party will assert.
2. The chronology of events.
3. The sequence that is most logical based on the hypothetical. The approaches that you have developed for each subject will help you to determine the organizational sequence.

Effective outlining for 10-15 minutes will greatly assist you when organizing your issues. To conserve time, remember to abbreviate words/phrases as much as possible in your outline. You should strive to learn proper outlining as demonstrated by the model outlines that accompany each of the hypotheticals presented in this book. At first, you may become frustrated with the technique because it is new to you. Do not let your frustration get in the way of your learning process. With practice, the outlining technique will become simple and reflexive.

Do not be fooled into thinking that the time spent outlining will detract from the time necessary to complete the final written answer. When done properly, outlining will afford you the opportunity to think through and strategize your analysis and organization before you commit yourself in the bluebook.

Outlining each issue as demonstrated, will enable you to separate major issues from minor issues, eliminate non-issues, adjust your organization when necessary, and determine how much time you must allocate to the writing of each issue. In essence, proper outlining will focus your analysis. This will ultimately save you time. For example, if you see on your outline that you have an issue that has multiple elements and facts, you will know that you will have to allocate more time to that issue than you will to another issue with fewer elements and facts.

Unless otherwise indicated, law school examinations must be completed within 60 minutes. You should strive to spend the first 10-20 minutes analyzing, organizing, and outlining before you begin writing in your bluebook

C. Writing

You must be able to demonstrate your ability to apply the elements of the applicable rule of law to facts in the hypothetical with a blend of precision and simplicity. The most efficient and effective method to accomplish this goal is through the use of the IRAC system. This method is thoroughly demonstrated in each model answer provided in this book.

To use the IRAC system, you should clearly indicate what the issue is in the form of a headnote. Follow the issue with the specific rule of law that applies. Then argue all applicable facts in relation to each and every element of the stated rule. If an element has a recognized "buzz word" associated with it, bring that "buzz word" into the discussion when addressing the facts that relate to that element.

When the analysis is completed, you must give a final conclusion. Because minimal point value is allocated to the conclusion, it should be no more than a one or two sentence summary of the stated issue.

EXAMPLE OF IRAC CRIMES ISSUE

(I) **Common Law Burglary Of The Stereo Equipment**

(R) Common law burglary is the (1) trespassory breaking and (2) entering of the (3) dwelling house of another in the (4) nighttime with the (5) specific intent to commit a felony therein.

(A) (1) Don will argue that when Oscar, the owner of the warehouse, gave him a duplicate key so that he could enter the warehouse (facts), his use of the key to gain access to the warehouse was with consent (buzz word). Thus, no trespassory breaking (element) and (2) entering (element). Further, (3) the warehouse is used for storage of stereo equipment (facts), not for the purposes of sleeping (buzz word) and, thus, is not the dwelling place of another (element). (4) The facts do not indicate that the entry (facts) was made in the nighttime (element) as required by common law.

(5) The State will rebut that Oscar and Don intended to remove the stereo equipment that Oscar normally sold, make it look like it "disappeared," sell it and then collect the "losses" from the insurance company (facts). His conduct (buzz word) demonstrates Don's specific intent to defraud the insurance company, a felony therein (element).

(C) However, due to the lack of a dwelling house and nighttime, it appears that the State will not be able to prove common law burglary of the stereo equipment.

The final written product should be completed within the remaining 40-50 minutes of the examination period. If you have analyzed and organized thoroughly, you should have no problem finishing the examination within the suggested time frame.

Strive for a bluebook that averages between 6-9 pages in length. Remember, it is the quality, not the quantity, of the written word that will establish success.

III. RECOMMENDED USE OF THE ESSAY EXAMINATION WRITING WORKBOOK

The First Year Essay Examination Writing Workbook is divided into the three substantive subject areas of Torts, Contracts, and Criminal Law. Each of these subjects is presented through five hypotheticals with corresponding model outlines and model answers.

Each hypothetical emphasizes a different area of the substantive law in the designated subject. Combined, the selected hypotheticals cover the entire subject and will expose the student to the issues and arguments most likely to be tested in Torts, Contracts, and Criminal Law during the first year of law school and on the State Bar Examination.

When proceeding through the materials presented in the First Year Essay Examination Writing Workbook, you will derive the optimum benefit by following these recommended steps:

1. Read the first hypothetical presented in the section designated "Torts". For the reasons discussed previously, be sure to fully understand the call of the question and the facts.

2. When you fully understand the facts, begin issue spotting. Use the IRAC outline worksheet provided. List the issues in the (I) column, the elements of each issue in the (R) column, the corresponding facts that prove or disprove each element in the (A) column, and the conclusion in the (C) column. With practice, this technique will become automatic. Review your outline. Add any further relevant data. Delete irrelevant data. Make organizational adjustments if necessary.

3. Upon completion of your outline, turn to the model outline provided. Compare your work. Identify the issues, elements and/or key facts that you have missed. Add those to your own outline. Compare your organization. Rethink your analysis if you find errors with your organization. Adjust your outline accordingly.

   You should constantly strive to produce outlines that are similar to the model outlines in this book. Abbreviate words and phrases on your outline wherever possible to conserve time. With practice, you will develop a form of shorthand that will make your outlining time more efficient.

4. Write your final answer in a bluebook using your outline as your guide. Write every issue in the IRAC format. Pay special attention to your analysis, always discussing the facts in relation to the individual elements of the rule. In this way, you will "usc the facts rather than merely repeating them."

5. Compare your written answer to the model answer provided. Identify inconsistencies in your IRAC. Review your analysis carefully in comparison to the model answer looking for weaknesses in factual discussion or missed analysis. Rewrite the analysis if you have missed major facts or arguments. Then proceed to the next hypothetical and repeat the process.

The first few hypotheticals should be analyzed, organized and written at your own pace without concern for the amount of time spent on the question. It will take practice to become familiar with the IRAC form of outlining and writing. Do not rush yourself.

As you proceed to the fifth or sixth hypothetical, you will become more proficient with the suggested techniques. At that point, you should begin to adhere to the time constraints imposed under examination conditions. You will then have an appreciation for the manner in which you must pace yourself to complete the exercise within the designated time period.

Do not expect to immediately articulate every argument as clearly as that demonstrated in the model answer. The ease upon which your legal writing skills develop will depend upon how much time you devote to practicing those skills. The more hypotheticals that you write, the more proficient your writing will become.

Practice is the essential ingredient that will help you develop the skills and confidence necessary to build the foundation for sound legal writing.

IV. PREPARING FOR LAW SCHOOL EXAMINATIONS

The key to performing well on law school examinations is preparation. Preparation involves a two prong process. First, you must learn the rules of law. Second, you must demonstrate how to apply those rules in the context of a factual hypothetical. Too many students make the mistake of placing all their emphasis on the first prong at the expense of the equally important second prong. The student who allows himself to fall into this trap usually produces essays that are too law oriented, conclusary, and weak in factual analysis. The First Year Essay Examination Writing Workbook will help you overcome these pitfalls.

Be sure to approach each hypothetical in this book as indicated. In this way, you will maximize the development of the skills that you must demonstrate for success in law school and on the Bar Examination.

GOOD LUCK!!

SECTION V

TORTS

TORTS

LEARN TO WRITE THE RIGHT WAY®

TORTS QUESTION #1

MASONS v. FINANCE COMPANY

Upon retirement, Bill and Jane Mason purchased a specially designed, custom-built mobile home trailer from Dealer for $65,000. They made a down payment of $10,000 and Dealer retained a security interest for the balance of the purchase price. The Masons moved with the mobile home into a space rented from Dream Park, where they paid monthly rental.

Several months later the trailer was removed from Dream Park by agents of Finance Company. Bill protested the removal and suffered a broken leg when he refused to step down and fell from the step of the trailer as it was being pulled away. He has since been hospitalized.

Because of mental distress suffered when she learned of these events, Jane has been hospitalized and under the care of a physician.

The trailer is now in the possession of Finance Company and is being advertised for sale.

Finance had erroneously repossessed the Mason's trailer, believing it was the property of Stranger. Stranger had defaulted on a debt due Finance that was secured by a mortgage on a trailer similar to the Mason's trailer.

The fair rental value of the Mason's trailer is $1,000 a month. A small section of the trailer was dented while it was in Finance's possession. It would cost $500 to repair the dent, but the damage is neither serious nor noticeable. The Mason's clothes and other personal possessions are missing from the trailer. The Mason's replaced such personal property at a cost of $5,000.

What are the rights of Bill and Jane, and what damages are available to them? Discuss.

IRAC OUTLINE SHEET

(I)	(R)	(A)	(C)

Model Outlines Serve As A Demonstration Only. Students Should Abbreviate Words & Phrases Whenever Possible To Keep Outline Time Between 15 - 20 Minutes.

EXAMPLE OF PROPER IRAC OUTLINE

MASON (M) v. FINANCE CO. (F)

(I)	(R)	(A)	(C)
RESPONDEAT SUPERIOR	Employer/Employee	Agents of F	Liable
	Course/Scope of Employment	Trailer removed from Dream Park	
TRESPASS TO LAND	Intentional	Trailer removed from Dream Park	Liable
	Interference	Repossessed	
	Land of Another	Mobile home/space rented/Dream Park Monthly rental paid – possession	
	No Consent/Privilege	Bill protested/refused to step down F erroneously repossessed trailer/ retained security interest F believed property of S who defaulted on loan/S's trailer similar to M's	
TRESPASS TO CHATTEL (trailer)	Intentional	(Mistake – privilege?) Trailer intentionally removed from Park	Liable
	Interference	Repossessed	
	Personal Property of Another	Mobile home/paid $65,000 with $10,000	
	No Consent/Privilege	F erroneously repossessed trailer/ F believed property of S – supra	
CONVERSION (trailer)	Intentional	Trailer removed supra	Liable
	Dominion/Control	Advertised for sale	
	Personal Property of Another	M purchased trailer for $65,000	
	No Consent/Privilege	Supra	
TRESPASS TO CHATTEL (clothes/personal possessions)	Intentional	Trailer removed supra	Liable
	Interference	Contents in trailer missing	
	Personal Property of Another	Clothes/personal possessions missing	
	No Consent/Privilege	Supra	
CONVERSION (clothes/personal possessions)	Intentional	Trailer removed supra	Liable
	Dominion/Control	Contents – supra	
	Personal Property of Another	Clothes/personal possessions missing	
	No Consent/Privilege	Supra	
ASSAULT	Intentional	Trailer removed supra	Arguable
	Apprehension	Bill protested/refused to step down/ trailer pulled away(?)	
	No Consent/Privilege	Supra	
BATTERY (Bill Mason)	Intentional	Trailer removed supra	Liable
	Harmful/Offensive Touching	Suffered broken leg when he refused to step down/fell from step of trailer as it was being pulled away/hospitalized	
	No Consent/Privilege	Supra	

(I)	(R)	(A)	(C)
INTENTIONAL INFLICTION OF EMOTIONAL DISTRESS (Bill Mason)	Intentional/Outrageous Conduct	Custom-built trailer removed/Bill protested/refused to step down	Arguable
	Calculated To/Does Cause	Erroneous repossession/fell from steps/ hospitalized	
	Severe Emotional Distress	Hospitalized	
NEGLIGENT INFLICTION OF EMOTIONAL DISTRESS (Jane Mason)	Duty Owed	F/check records properly/security interest in Stranger's trailer/Jane wife	Arguable
	Foreseeable Risk/Injury	Bill's injury/erroneous repossession hospitalized/under care of physician	
	Foreseeable Result	Learned of events/mental distress Suffered/loss of custom trailer/Bill's hospitalization	
COMPENSATORY DAMAGES	Damages Naturally Flowing	$500 repair dented trailer but not serious, noticeable (Forced sale?) $65,00 trailer/$10,000 down/$1,000 per mo./rental value of space Personal possessions missing/replaced at $5,000 Medical expenses/pain and suffering Bill hospitalized/Jane suffered mental distress/hospitalized	CompensatoryDamages
PUNITIVE DAMAGES	Willful/Wanton Conduct	Erroneously repossessed/through it was S who had defaulted on loan/S's trailer similar to M's/(recklessness?) Battery/emotional distress supra	Arguable

EXAMPLE OF IRAC TORTS ISSUE

(I) **Trespass To Land**

(R) Trespass to land is (1) the intentional interference with (2) the land in possession of another (3) without consent or privilege.

(A) The Masons will assert that when Finance Company's agents removed their trailer from Dream Park, such conduct was done with a substantial certainly to intrude on the rental space where the trailer was located in order to repossess it. Such an invasion constituted (1) an intentional interference. Even though the Masons did not own the land, the fact that they rented it gave them exclusive possessery rights to the property sufficient to show (2) land in possession of another.

Bill protested the removal of the trailer and refused to step down from it, which clearly demonstrated his (3) lack of consent.

Finance Company will rebut that they had retained a security interest in the trailer, which gave them the privilege to repossess the trailer when payments were not made.

However, the removal of the Masons' trailer from their space was due to Finance Company's erroneous belief that it belonged to Stranger who had defaulted on his loan. Despite the fact that Stranger's trailer looked similar, Finance Company's (4) privilege would not extend to the mistaken repossession of the Masons' trailer.

(C) Finance Company will be liable for trespass to land.

The agents' conduct of pulling the trailer away while Bill was still on the step was substantially certain to cause actual physical contact when he fell. Thus, it was an intentional act. In fact, Bill did fall and break his leg, which required hospitalization, clearly demonstrating a harmful and offensive touching. As previously discussed, there was no consent or privilege for the agents acts.

Finance Company will be liable for battery.

Intentional Infliction of Emotional Distress (Bill Mason)

Intentional infliction of emotional distress is the intentional outrageous conduct by the defendant which is calculated to cause and which does cause severe emotional distress.

Bill will assert that the removal of his custom-built trailer while he was on the step, despite his protest and refusal to step down from the trailer, exceeded the bounds of decent behavior and was intentional, outrageous conduct.

Further, repossession of one's home is always calculated to cause distress. The outrageous nature of doing so erroneously and without justification would be the indicia of Bill's emotional distress. Since Agents' reckless conduct was calculated to cause mental anguish, Bill's subsequent hospitalization would suffice for recovery.

Finance Company will be liable to Bill for intentional infliction of emotional distress.

Negligent Infliction of Emotional Distress - (Jane Mason)

A duty is owed to exercise due care not to subject others to a foreseeable risk of physical injury that might foreseeably cause emotional distress.

Jane will contend that the Finance Company owed a duty of care to document and review its records carefully before repossessing a trailer from a defaulting debtor.

The facts indicate that it failed to properly identify Stranger's trailer, which resulted in the erroneous repossession, of the Masons' trailer. Thus, Finance Company's conduct equated to a lack of due care subjecting Jane to a foreseeable risk of injury.

Since Jane was Bill's wife, it was foreseeable that she would suffer mental distress upon learning of the events of both the repossession of their custom-built trailer containing their personal possessions, and of Bill's hospitalization. Thus, her emotional anguish was a foreseeable result of Finance Company's conduct.

Finance Company will be liable to Jane for negligent infliction of emotional distress.

Compensatory Damages

Compensatory damages are those that naturally flow from the wrong and such as will make good or replace the loss caused by the wrong or injury sustained.

The trailer was dented. Even though the damage was not serious or noticeable, the Masons will assert that they are entitled to have the trailer put back in the condition it was in before the repossession. Thus, they will seek the $500 it will cost for repair.

In the alternative, as discussed supra under Conversion, the Masons may demand that Finance Company pay them the value of the trailer as a forced sale rather than accept its return.

Further, the Masons will establish that they lost the use of their $65,000 trailer and the value of the trailer rental space for which they paid $1,000 per month. They will seek to be reimbursed for reasonable rental value for the period of dispossession due to their loss of use.

The Masons will also seek reimbursement for the $5,000 that they were forced to spend to replace the clothes and personal possessions that were missing after the repossession.

They will ask for reimbursement for all medical expenses incurred during their hospitalization for the treatment of the physical and emotional injuries sustained supra. As all of the above stated damages naturally flowed from the repossession, the court should allow the specified amounts.

Compensatory damages will be awarded.

Punitive Damages

Punitive damages are those damages awarded to the plaintiff where the wrong complained of was aggravated by willful, wanton acts of the defendant.

Finance Company repossessed the Masons trailer as a result of its erroneous belief that it belonged to Stranger. Stranger's trailer was similar to the Masons'. However, the repossession, even though a mistake, was still wrongful. Nevertheless, their conduct, under the circumstances, was not so gross as to equate to willful wanton conduct.

However, Agents' conduct regarding their battery and emotional distress to Bill, as discussed supra, may be viewed by the court as willful and wanton, sufficient for a recovery of punitive damages.

It's a close question as to whether punitive damages will be awarded in this situation.

TORTS QUESTION #2

BESS v. JIM

Jim was a bachelor who lived on the second floor of an apartment house. Early one stormy morning, Jim detected the smell of gas and discovered that the pilot light on his water heater had gone out and that gas was escaping. Since Jim could not stop the flow of gas, had no telephone and was late for work, he knocked on the door of his friend Fred, who occupied the adjoining apartment, and told Fred of the trouble. He asked Fred to phone the gas company and ask it to repair the leaking heater as soon as possible. Fred, who was suffering from a bad head cold, assured Jim that he would notify the company at once. After Jim left, Fred became interested in a television program and forgot to notify the gas company.

During the day gas accumulated in Jim's apartment. Late in the afternoon, Bess, Jim's girlfriend, approached the door to his apartment. She was smoking a marijuana cigarette in violation of a criminal statute. As she opened the door with the key Jim had given her, there was a violent explosion and Bess sustained serious injuries.

The explosion shook the wall separating Jim and Fred's apartments. Fred had just admitted Dolores, who had come to his apartment soliciting for the March of Dimes. The sound of the explosion and the shaking of the wall so frightened Dolores, who was recuperating from a nervous breakdown, that she jumped out the window and was injured when she struck the pavement.

A labor strike was in progress at the gas company and the company was only able to answer about half of its emergency calls during the course of the day.

What are the rights of Bess and Dolores against Jim? Discuss.

What are the rights of Bess and Dolores against Fred? Discuss.

IRAC OUTLINE SHEET

(I)	(R)	(A)	(C)

EXAMPLE OF PROPER IRAC OUTLINE

BESS v. JIM

(I)	(R)	(A)	(C)
NEGLIGENCE	Special Duty Landowner/Occupier Invitee/Licensee	Jim lived in apt. (occupier) Bess girlfriend- given key to apt.	Liable
	Breach	Left apt. with gas leaking Could not stop flow Late for work No phone Asked Fred to call Gas co. Fred assured he would	
	Causation Actual Proximate	But for Jim's negligence Injuries caused by explosion from leaking gas-foreseeable Fred sick, watching TV, forgot to call-unforeseeable	
	Damages	Serious bodily injury	
CONTRIBUTORY NEGLIGENCE VIOLATION OF STATUTE	Conduct Below Standard of Care	Smoking marijuana	No Contribution Negligence
	Contributing Cause of injury	Violated city ordinance Cigarette caused explosion	
	Intent Class Injury	Criminal marijuana statute Drug victims? Explosion (?)	

DOLORES v. JIM

(I)	(R)	(A)	(C)
NEGLIGENCE	Special Duty Landowner/Occupier Licensee	Jim apartment occupier Dolores solicitor for March of Dimes Admitted to Fred's apartment	Liable
	General Duty Zone of Danger	Leaking Gas Solicitor in apartment	
	Breach	Supra	
	Causation Actual Proximate	Supra Leaking gas Injuries to solicitor Shaking wall Nervous condition-(thin skull)	
	Damages	Injuries when struck pavement	
NEGLIGENT INFLICTION OF EMOTIONAL DISTRESS	Duty Owed	Solicitor	Liable
	Foreseeable Risk/Injury	Leaking gas/injuries	
	Foreseeable Result	Explosion Fright Jumped out Fred's window Recovering from nervous breakdown	

BESS v. FRED

(I)	(R)	(A)	(C)
NEGLIGENCE	General Duty	Fred assured Jim he'd call Gas Co Explosion in Jim's Apt not Fred's Gas Co on strike	Not Liable

(I)	(R)	(A)	(C)
DOLORES v. FRED			
NEGLIGENCE	Special Duty Landowner/Occupier Licensee	Fred lived in apartment Given permission to enter March of Dimes	Not Liable
	Breach	Failed to warn	
	Causation Actual	 But for failure to warn (?) Just admitted to Dolores to apartment	
	Proximate	∅	
	Damages	∅	

EXAMPLE OF IRAC TORTS ISSUE

(I) **Negligent Infliction Of Emotional Distress**

(R) (1) A duty is owed to exercise due care not to subject others to (2) a foreseeable risk of physical injury that might (3) foreseeably result in emotional distress.

(A) Jim had (1) a duty to eliminate the danger from the leaking gas so that Dolores would not be subjected to (2) the risk of physical injury from an explosion.

Further, it is foreseeable that when she was exposed to a gas explosion, she would become so frightened that she would possibly jump out a window in order to escape, especially since she was recuperating from a nervous breakdown.

Jim will counter that Dolores was in an adjacent apartment and was never subjected to either actual physical impact or the threat of immediate physical impact. Therefore, (3) since there was no risk of actual physical injury, it was not foreseeable that Dolores would experience injuries.

However, the shock to her nervous condition has been held sufficient to establish physical harm. This shock caused her to jump from the window and sustain physical injuries.

(C) Therefore, Dolores' emotional distress was foreseeably caused by Jim's negligence.

SUGGESTED MODEL ANSWER

BESS v. JIM

Negligence

Negligence requires a showing that a duty was owed, that the duty was breached, and that the breach was the actual and proximate cause of damages.

Special Duty - Land Occupier

Jim lived in the apartment where the explosion occurred and, therefore, he was a land occupier. Bess was Jim's girlfriend to whom he had given a key to the apartment as an implied invitation to use the premises. The availability of the apartment to Bess was related to Jim's interest in the relationship. Therefore, she was Jim's invitee.

Because she was an invitee, Jim owed her a special duty to inspect and discover the source of the leaking gas and to warn her of its known danger and fix it so she would not be exposed to an unreasonable risk of harm.

Jim will counter that Bess was a social guest who was visiting his apartment for reasons unrelated to his business interests. She was, therefore, a licensee. As such, he would owe her only a duty to warn of known dangerous conditions.

Whether she is determined to be a licensee or invitee, Jim owed her, at a minimum, a duty to warn of the known danger of the gas leak of which he was aware before he left the apartment.

Therefore, Jim owes a special duty of due care to Bess.

Breach

Since Jim left the apartment knowing that the gas was leaking without taking action to fix it himself, he did not act as a reasonable man under the same or similar circumstances. His failure to warn her of the dangerous condition was a further breach of his duty of due care.

Jim will counter that he could not stop the gas flow. He asked Fred to call the Gas Company for him. He had relied on Fred's assurance that he would do so. He had no phone and was late for work making it impossible for him to warn Bess. Therefore, he did not breach his duty.

However, the duty to warn was a nondelegable duty. He should have posted a warning on the door. Jim's attempt to delegate the responsibility to Fred was, itself, a breach.

Actual Causation

"But for" Jim's failure to notify the Gas Company or warn of the leak, Bess would not have been injured.

Thus, Jim was the actual cause of her injuries.

Proximate Causation

Absent a warning, it was foreseeable that the leaking gas could be ignited and explode, causing injuries to persons on or near the premises.

Jim will rebut that the cause of the explosion was Fred's failure to call the Gas Company. Had he done so, the dangerous conditions would not have existed and a warning would not have be necessary. Fred's forgetfulness was unforeseeable because he had promised that he would do so. Therefore, this would break the chain of causation.

However, Fred's promise was gratuitous which created no legal duty on his part to call. It was foreseeable that he would forget to call since he was watching TV, was sick and couldn't smell the leaking gas.

Further, since mere negligence is always deemed foreseeable, Fred's forgetfulness will not sever chain of causation.

Therefore, Jim was the proximate cause of Bess' injuries.

Damages

Bess sustained serious bodily injuries as a result of the explosion. Therefore, she would have no problem proving damages.

Defense Contributory Negligence - Violation of Statute

Contributory negligence is measured by a plaintiff's conduct which falls below the standard of care to which he/she is required to conform for his/her own protection, and which contributes to his/her own injury.

If Bess hadn't been smoking marijuana in violation of the city ordinance, the explosion would not have occurred. Her conduct was both dangerous and illegal. It fell below the standard of care to which Bess was required to conform to for her own protection.

Bess will counter that the intent of the ordinance was to protect people from drug trafficking related to marijuana smoking. Bess was not within the class of persons i.e., victims, sought to be protected from this criminal activity.

Furthermore, it was not within the contemplation of the legislature to prevent injuries from explosion caused by persons smoking marijuana cigarettes. Her violation did not contribute to her injuries.

Based on the foregoing, the violation of the statute will not support a defense of contributory negligence.

DOLORES v. JIM

Negligence

Negligence as defined supra.

Special Duty - Land Occupier

Dolores will assert that Jim was a land occupier (supra). She had been given permission to enter the apartment premises to collect money for the March of Dimes and was therefore a licensee (supra). Thus, Jim owed her a special duty to warn of the known gas leak or make it safe.

However, Fred had given Dolores permission to enter Fred's apartment, not Jim's. She was not Jim's licensee. Therefore, he owed her no special duty.

General Duty

Jim owed Dolores a general duty of due care not to expose her to unreasonable risks of harm from leaking gas. In this case, he owed a duty to everyone in the apartment complex to eliminate the danger.

Jim will counter that Dolores was a solicitor. He had no way of knowing that she would be within the zone of danger since she did not live on the premises. Therefore, he owed her no duty.

However, Jim's duty of due care was owed to all persons who would foreseeably be on the apartment premises. March of Dimes representatives often solicit funds from tenants in apartment complexes, and therefore, their presence is foreseeable.

Jim would thus owe her a general duty of due care.

Breach

As discussed supra under Bess v. Jim.

Actual Causation

As discussed supra under Bess v. Jim.

Proximate Causation

When one leaves leaking gas in an unoccupied apartment, it is foreseeable that solicitors in the complex can be injured.

Jim will rebut that it is not foreseeable that Dolores would jump out the window after hearing an explosion in an adjoining apartment. The most that would be foreseeable would be minor injury from falling plaster from the shaking wall. Therefore, Dolores' reaction was unforeseeable sufficient to sever liability.

However, because Dolores was frightened by the explosion , she reacted as a woman with a nervous condition would in a similar situation. Thus, even though the sequence of events leading up to her injuries may have been unforeseeable, the result, i.e., bodily injury, was foreseeable.

Under the tort theory of the thin skulled plaintiff, Jim must take his victim as he finds her. Since it is the foreseeability of the result which determines liability, Dolores appears to have the stronger argument.

Therefore, Jim was the proximate cause of her injuries.

Damages

Jim will be liable for Dolores' injuries sustained when she struck the pavement.

Negligent Infliction of Emotional Distress

A duty is owed to exercise due care not to subject others to a foreseeable risk of physical injury that might foreseeably result in emotional distress.

Jim had a duty to eliminate the danger from the leaking gas so that Dolores would not be subjected to the risk of physical injury from an explosion.

Further, it is foreseeable that when she was exposed to a gas explosion , she would become so frightened that she would possibly jump out a window in order to escape, especially since she was recuperating from a nervous breakdown.

Jim will counter that Dolores was in an adjacent apartment and was never subjected to either actual physical impact or the threat of immediate physical impact. Therefore, since there was no risk of actual physical injury it was not foreseeable that Dolores would experience injuries.

However, the shock to her nervous condition has been held sufficient to establish physical harm. This shock caused her to jump from the window and sustain physical injuries.

Therefore, Dolores' emotional distress was foreseeably caused by Jim's negligence.

BESS v. FRED

Negligence

Negligence as defined supra.

Duty

Fred had assured Jim that he would call the Gas Company at once so that persons in the complex would not be exposed to an unreasonable risk of harm from exploding gas. Therefore, his promise created a general duty of due care.

However, Fred will counter that his promise was gratuitous. He did not cause the leak or the explosion, and his apartment was not involved in the accident. Furthermore, even if he had called the Gas Company, they would not have responded because of the strike. Therefore, he owed no duty to Bess.

Fred's argument appears to be the stronger and Bess will have no cause of action.

DOLORES v. FRED

Negligence

Negligence as defined supra.

Special Duty - Licensee

Fred lived in the apartment adjacent to Jim's and, thus, was a land occupier. He had given her permission to enter his apartment so that he could donate to the March of Dimes. Therefore, Dolores was a licensee.

Further, since Fred knew of the danger from the leaking gas in Jim's apartment, owed her a duty to warn her of the possibility of explosion.

Breach

When Fred failed to warn Dolores, he did not act as a reasonable man in the same or similar circumstances. Therefore, he breached his duty.

Actual Causation

"But for" Fred's failure to warn, she would not have been injured.

Fred will counter that he "had just admitted" Dolores to his apartment. Even if he had warned her, she wouldn't have had time to get out before the explosion. She would have been injured with or without a warning.

Therefore his negligence was not the actual cause of her injuries.

Dolores will not be able to recover against Fred.

TORTS QUESTION #3

ACE AUTO RENTALS

An automobile, owned by Ace Auto Rentals (Ace) and rented to and driven by Bruce, collided with an automobile owned and driven by Chuck, when Chuck entered a main highway without looking to see if it was safe. Bruce would have been able to avoid the collision except that he was driving at a recklessly high speed. Unknown to Ace, Bruce had no driver's license.

Chuck's car caught fire. Dave, a passenger who had met Chuck through a want ad and was sharing expenses and driving responsibilities while on a cross country trip, escaped without injury. Chuck was trapped in the burning car. Peter, a bystander, tried to pull Chuck out of the car. Peter was severely burned. Chuck died of his burns.

What are Peter's rights, if any, against Ace, Dave, and Chuck's estate? Discuss.

IRAC OUTLINE SHEET

(I)	(R)	(A)	(C)

EXAMPLE OF PROPER IRAC OUTLINE

PETER (P) v. ACE (A)

(I)	(R)	(A)	(C)
VICARIOUS LIABILITY	Bailor - Chattel Generally Not Vicariously Liable	A auto rental A owner rented car to B	No Liability
	Bailee's Conduct	B driving recklessly/high speed	
	Failure to Exercise Due Care	Unknown to A	
	Bailee's Selection	B no license	
NEGLIGENCE	Duty	A auto rental agency (Standard of care?) B rented car from A/qualified driver? (Duty of due care?) Unknown to A,B had no license	Liable
	Breach	Failure to check (Reasonable?)	
	Causation Actual	But for failure to check B has no license and	
	Proximate	B driving recklessly C entered main highway without looking to see if safe (foreseeable?) B would have avoided C if not driving recklessly	
	Damages	Severe burns	

PETER v. DAVE (D)

(I)	(R)	(A)	(C)
NEGLIGENCE	Duty	P passenger in C's car (Duty to control C's driving?)	No Liability
VICARIOUS LIABILITY JOINT VENTURE	Agreement to Engage Joint	D answered C's ad	Split of Jurisdictions
	Enterprise	D passenger in C's car C/D agreed to share expenses/ driving responsibilities	
	Common Purpose	C/D on cross country trip (business?)	
	Equal Right Management/ Control	Auto owned/driven by C Sharing expenses/driving supra	

PETER v. CHUCK'S ESTATE (C)

(I)	(R)	(A)	(C)
SURVIVAL STATUTE	Tort Survives Death of Tortfeasor	P tried to pull C from burning car P seriously injured due to C's negligence C died – Estate may be liable	Valid
NEGLIGENCE	Duty	C entered main highways w/o looking supra P bystander	Liable
	Breach	See facts under duty (reasonable)	
	Causation Actual Proximate	But for failure to look Entered before looking B's reckless driving (foreseeable?)	
	Damages	Severely burned	

(I)	(R)	(A)	(C)
DEFENSE: CONTRIBUTORY NEGLIGENCE	Conduct – Below Standard of Care	P tried to pull C from burning car C trapped in car	No Defense
	Contributing Cause of Injury	P severely burned/death (Public policy/rescuer)	
DEFENSE: ASSUMPTION OF THE RISK	Known/Appreciated Risk	Burning car	No Defense
	Voluntary Encountered	C trapped in burning car (Public policy/rescuer)	

EXAMPLE OF IRAC TORTS ISSUE

(I) **Defense: Contributory Negligence**

(R) Contributory negligence is measured by a plaintiff's (1) conduct, which falls below the standard of care to which he/she is required to conform for his/her own protection and (2) which contributes to his/her own injury.

(A) Chuck's estate will contend that when Peter attempted to pull Chuck's body from the burning car, he placed himself in extreme and obvious danger. The act of doing so was (1) conduct below the standard of care to which Peter should have conformed to protect his own safety. (2) It contributed to his own severe burns.

However, danger to others invites rescue which public policy encourages when reasonable. Peter saw hat Chuck was trapped. His attempt to save Chuck's life by pulling him from the burning car was what any reasonable person would have done under the same or similar circumstances. Public policy will not penalize the act of a "Good Samaritan" under these circumstances.

(C) Therefore, contributory negligence is no defense.

SUGGESTED MODEL ANSWER

PETER v. ACE

Vicarious Liability

A bailor of chattel will generally not be vicariously liable for the tortious act of a bailee even if he has failed to exercise due care in the bailee's selection.

Ace Auto Rentals (Ace) was in the business of renting its automobiles. As such, Ace was a bailor of chattel. When Ace accepted Bruce's business by renting one of its cars to him, Ace did not vicariously assume the responsibility for Bruce's reckless high speed driving which was a tortious act.

Although Bruce's lack of a driver's license was "unknown to Ace," Ace's failure to check for a license as a minimum qualification for a car rental equated to a lack of due care. This failure directly resulted in Bruce's selection as a bailee of the rental auto.

However, since the negligence of the bailee is not impuded to the bailor, Ace will not be held vicariously liable for the damage caused by Bruce.

Negligence

Negligence requires that a duty was owed, that the duty was breached and the breach was the actual and proximate cause of damages.

Duty

As a rental agency, Ace had a duty to determine whether Bruce, a prospective renter, was reasonable qualified to drive its vehicles. Verification of Bruce's valid driver's license would constitute the normal standard of care in the rental industry. This duty was owed to all other user of the highways so as not to expose them to an unreasonable risk of harm from unlicensed or reckless drivers. Since Peter was a bystander on the main highway where Ace's rental car was being driven by Bruce, he was a foreseeable plaintiff to whom the duty was owed.

Breach

Even though Ace did not know that Bruce had no driver's license, if its employees had taken the time to check, they would have discovered this fact. When Ace rented an automobile to Bruce before determining whether Bruce was a qualified, licensed driver, it failed to act as an average reasonable rental agency under the same of similar circumstances.

Therefore, Ace breached its duty of due care.

Actual Causation

"But for" Ace's failure to check Bruce for a driver's license, Bruce would not have been able to rent a car in which to recklessly drive.

Ace was the actual cause of the accident.

Proximate Causation

Peter will assert that when an automobile rental agency fails to check a renter for a driver's license, it is foreseeable that the car will be rented to an unlicensed driver who may be reckless in the use of the automobile resulting in injuries to others.

Ace will counter that Bruce's high speed reckless driving was gross conduct unrelated to his lack of a driver's license. His conduct was an independent intervening act that should break the chain of causation.

Further, Chuck's conduct of entering the main highway without looking to see if it was safe was an independent intervening act that would break the direct chain of causation between Bruce's negligence and Peter's injuries.

However, even if it is independent, reckless driving on the part of an unlicensed driver is foreseeable. A person who fails to conform to the minimum requirement of having a valid driver's license when operating a vehicle, will probably have less regard for adhering to the standards of driving safety necessary to protect that license and others on the road.

Even though Chuck's conduct may have been an intervening act, the negligence of other drivers is also always foreseeable. The accident fell within the foreseeable risk of injury to Peter. It appears to be a dependent, normal response to Bruce's negligence which could have been avoided if Bruce had not been driving recklessly.

Ace is the proximate cause of Peter's injuries.

Damages

Peter was severely burned when he attempted to pull Chuck from the burning vehicle after the accident. These bodily injuries would constitute damages for which he would seek compensation.

PETER v. DAVE

Negligence

Defined supra.

Duty

Peter will argue that as a passenger in Chuck's car, Dave owed a duty of due care to insure driver safety by warning Chuck to look before entering the main highway.

However, the car was owned and driven by Chuck. It was in no way under the control or direction of Dave. As a passenger, Dave had no duty to advise Chuck in the operation of the car. There are no facts to indicate that Chuck's driving was either encouraged by Dave or, in any way, excessive or unusually reckless which could give rise to a duty.

Therefore, Dave owed no duty of due care under the circumstances.

Vicarious Liability/Joint Venture

Persons who engage in a joint enterprise are vicariously liable for the conduct of the other members within the scope of that enterprise, if an agreement exists between two or more persons to engage in a common purpose with equal right of voice and control.

Dave answered Chuck's ad and agreed with him to share expenses and driving responsibilities while on a cross-country trip. Thus, a mutual right to management and control in the operation of the vehicle arose. As such, Chuck and Dave were engaged in a joint enterprise.

Chuck and Dave's common purpose was to make the cross-country trip.

The car was owned and driven by Chuck at the time of the accident. However, Peter will assert that sharing expenses and driving responsibilities would equate to equal right of voice and control for Dave even when he was not personally driving the automobile.

Dave will counter that he had merely answered an ad to secure transportation for a trip across country. The agreement to share costs and driving responsibilities was intended to save money and physical strength during the long trip. Such a purpose was meant to fulfill personal economic needs rather than for the purposes of business. Since a split of jurisdictions exists as to whether a business purpose is required, Dave may have a strong argument.

Depending upon the jurisdiction, so will determine whether vicarious liability will apply.

PETER v. CHUCK'S ESTATE

Survival Statute

Survival statutes permit causes of action for personal and property damages to survive the death of the tortfeasor.

Peter was attempting to rescue Chuck from the accident caused by Chuck's negligence. He was seriously burned when he tried to pull Chuck out of his car. If he can show that his medical expenses would have been recoverable from Chuck had Chuck lived infra, he may recover from Chuck's estate.

Therefore, Chuck's conduct may render his estate liable.

Negligence

Defined supra.

Duty

As a driver on the main highway, Chuck owed a duty of due care to look before entering a main highway to see if it was safe so as not to expose other users to an unreasonable risk of harm. Even though Peter was a bystander, he was legitimately using that highway and was a foreseeable plaintiff to whom the duty was owed.

Breach

When Chuck entered the main highway without looking to see if it was safe, he did not act as an average reasonable man under the same or similar circumstances.

Therefore, Chuck breached his duty of due care.

Actual Causation

"But for" Chuck's failure to look before entering the highway, the accident would not have occurred.

Chuck is the actual cause of the accident.

Proximate Causation

When Chuck entered the main highway before looking, it was foreseeable that it might not be safe. Doing so would directly cause a possible accident with resulting injuries.

Chuck's estate will contend that Bruce's act of negligence (supra) was an independent intervening act which was unforeseeable sufficient to break the chain of causation.

However, reckless and high speed driving on highways is always conduct that should be anticipated. Although it may be an intervening act, it was foreseeable and will not break the chain of causation.

Chuck's negligence was the proximate cause of the accident.

Damages

Discussed supra. Chuck's estate will be liable for Peter's injuries caused by Chuck's negligence.

Defenses: Contributory Negligence

Contributory negligence is measured by a plaintiff's conduct which falls below the standard of care to which he/she is required to conform for his/her own protection and which contributes to his/her own injury.

Chuck's estate will contend that when Peter attempted to pull Chuck's body from the burning car, he placed himself in extreme and obvious danger. The act of doing so was conduct below the standard of care to which Peter should have conformed to protect his own safety. It contributed to his own severe burns and death.

However, danger to others invites rescue which public policy encourages when reasonable. Peter saw that Chuck was trapped. His attempt to save Chuck's life by pulling him from the burning car was what any reasonable person would have done under the same or similar circumstances. Public policy will not penalize the act of a "good samaritan" under these circumstances.

Therefore, contributory negligence is no defense.

Assumption of Risk

One who knows and appreciates a known danger and voluntarily chooses to encounter it will have assumed the risk of injury.

Even though Peter may have known that pulling Chuck from a burning car could endanger his own life, he was acting in an emergency. His intent was to save a life, not voluntarily encounter the risk of danger if there had been another alternative. Since Peter was a rescuer, public policy will not impose liability for the act of a "good samaritan."

Assumption of the risk is no defense.

Note to students regarding the doctrine of last clear chance

It appears from the facts that Bruce could have avoided the accident if he hadn't been driving recklessly. However, since the actions of Bruce, as a defendant, were not asked for in the call of the question, it has no applicability to this lawsuit. The call would have had to request a discussion of negligence under the lawsuit of Ace v Bruce in order for the doctrine to apply.

TORTS QUESTION #4

GLORIA v. TINTCO/MAG

Mag, Inc. publishes a magazine and operates a laboratory for testing merchandise of its advertisers. Mag authorizes the use of a symbol that says "Mag Seal of Approval" when Mag's tests indicate the product is safe and wholesome.

Mag examined samples of Tint hair coloring produced by Tintco, Inc.. Mag's tests indicated that Tint was effective and satisfactory. Mag authorized Tintco to use Mag's Seal of Approval in advertising Tint and on Tintco's labels placed on containers of Tint. Neither Tintco nor Mag was aware that when Tint is brought into direct contact with Balm, an infrequently used scalp medicine, Tint causes hair to turn purple.

Gloria, a contestant in a beauty contest, used Tint on her hair while it was still wet with Balm. As a result, Gloria's hair turned purple and she had to withdraw from the contest. She had been regarded as the favorite. To Gloria's embarrassment her hair discoloration persisted until her hair grew out.

What are Gloria's rights against:

1. Tintco? Discuss.
2. Mag? Discuss.

IRAC OUTLINE SHEET

(I)	(R)	(A)	(C)

EXAMPLE OF PROPER IRAC OUTLINE

GLORIA (G) v TINTCO (T)

(I)	(R)	(A)	(C)
PRODUCTS LIABILITY	Manufacture/Supplier	T produced Tint	Theories May Apply
	Product	Tint hair coloring	
NEGLIGENCE	Duty	Tint produced by T (inspect/warn?) G – foreseeable user of Tint	Liable
	Breach	G used Tint/hair turned purple T not aware that Tint in direct contact with Balm causes hair to turn purple (warning defect?) (Design defect – inadequate testing?) Balm an infrequently used scalp medicine (reasonable inspection?)	
	Causation Actual	But for failure – supra Tint/Balm contact	
	Proximate	T's lack of knowledge Tint/Balm contact (foreseeable?) Balm infrequently used	
	Damages (Generals)	G, a beauty contestant, used Tint G's hair turned purple Embarrassment until hair grew out	
	(Specials)	G had to withdraw from beauty contest/ had been regarded favorite	
EXPRESS WARRANTY	Representation	T used Mag's seal of approval in advertising and on container labels Seal indicates product safe/wholesome	Liable
	Commercial Seller	Tintco produced Tint	
	Buyer Reliance	G used Tint on her hair	
	Damages	Hair turned purple	
IMPLIED WARRANTY (MERCHANTABILITY)	Fair/Average Quality	Tint in contact with Balm made hair turn purple (fit for normal use?)	Liable
	Damages	Facts supra	
IMPLIED WARRANTY (FITNESS FOR INTENDED PURPOSE)	Seller Knows Of Buyer's Use	T produced Tint for hair coloring	Liable
	Buyer Reliance On Seller Skill/ Judgment	G beauty contestant/used Tint of hair	
	Damages	Facts supra	
STRICT LIABILITY IN TORT	Defective Product Restatement 402A – Unreasonably Dangerous California – Harmful In Intended Use	T produced Tint G used/hair turned purple T not aware Tint in contact with Balm caused purple hair (defective design/warning?)	Liable
	Defective Existence	Sold without warning	
	Causation Actual Proximate	Facts supra under negligence Facts supra under negligence	
	Damages	Facts supra under negligence	

GLORIA v. MAG (M)

(I)	®	(A)	©
NEGLIGENT MISREPRESENTATION	Misrepresentation of Material Fact	M seal of approval/product safe/ effective/satisfactory/wholesome Tint with Balm caused hair to turn purple	Liable
	Lack Of Due Care	M not aware that Tint with Balm causes purple hair	
	Induces justifiable Reliance	G used Tint – Purchaser	
	Damages	G's hair turned purple	
NEGLIGENCE	Duty	M publishes magazine/operates lab for testing advertisers products Authorize seal of approval when tests shows product safe/wholesome (Gloria – foreseeable plaintiff?)	Liable
	Breach	M not aware that Tint with Balm cases purple hair (Inadequate testing?)	
	Causation		
	Actual	Seal/facts supra under negligence -- products	
	Proximate	Seal/facts supra under negligence – products	
	Damages (General)	Facts supra under negligence -- products	

EXAMPLE OF IRAC TORTS ISSUE

(I) **Negligent Misrepresentation**

(R) Negligent misrepresentation is (1) the misrepresentation of a material fact made with a (2) lack of due care which (3) induces the justifiable reliance of the plaintiff causing (4) damages.

(A) Mag's Seal of Approval which indicated that Tint was safe, effective and wholesome when, in fact, it caused hair to turn purple when used with Balm, was (1) a misrepresentation of a material fact. Since Mag was unaware of this side effect at the time it authorized its Seal of Approval, the misrepresentation was made with a (2) lack of due care.

It is reasonable to infer that the Seal of Approval may have played a substantial part in inducing Gloria to use Tint. If it did, her (3) actual reliance on its safety and effectiveness was justifiable. Gloria's purple hair would demonstrate (4) damages.

(C) Mag will be liable for negligent misrepresentation.

SUGGESTED MODEL ANSWER

1. GLORIA v. TINTCO

Products Liability

When a product causes injury, the manufacturer may be liable under one or more of the theories of recovery governed by Products Liability.

Tintco produced Tint, a hair coloring. As the manufacturer and supplier of the product, Tintco will be held liable for damages caused by the use of its product if it is proven to be defective under one or more of the theories of recovery governed by Products Liability.

Negligence - Duty

A manufacturer owes a duty of due care to all persons who may be foreseeably injured by negligence in the manufacture of a defective product. Common law extended due care only to those in privity of contract (**Winterbottom v. Wright**). Modern law extends liability to all foreseeable users (**McPherson v Buick**).

Tintco produced Tint, a hair coloring. As the manufacturer, Tintco owed a duty of due care to inspect, discover and correct any defects associated with the use of Tint to insure its safety and eliminate harm from the product. Tintco had a further duty to exercise due care to warn potential users of all dangers, risks, or side effects that could develop from its use.

Because Gloria purchased and used Tint, she was a foreseeable consumer.

Therefore, Tintco owed a duty to Gloria.

Breach

When Gloria used Tint while her hair was still wet with Balm, her hair turned purple. Thus, Tint was defective. There was no warning of this risk on the product label. As an average reasonable consumer, she would not expect such a drastic side effect and, therefore, Tint did not meet her ordinary commercial expectations.

Tintco will counter that Balm was an infrequently used scalp medication. As such, Tintco's failure to discover and warn of the unlikely risk of the combined use of Tint and Balm was reasonable under the circumstances.

However, even though Balm may have been an infrequently used scalp medicine, it was a known hair product sold on the open market. Tintco should have tested its compatibility with Tint before selling it on that same market. Had it done so, Tintco would have been aware that direct contact between the two products would cause hair to turn purple. It could have then warned users of this risk.

Further Gloria would contend that due to Tintco's inadequate testing supra, Tint was, at a minimum, defective in design.

Therefore, Tintco breached its duty of due care to Gloria.

Actual Causation

"But for" Tintco's failure to adequately test and warn of the effect of Tint when used in direct contact with Balm, Gloria's hair would not have turned purple.

Tintco is the actual cause of Gloria's damages.

Proximate Causation

When a producer of a hair coloring product fails to adequately test its product with other known hair product and fails to warn consumers of all potential side effects, damages to the hair are a foreseeable result.

Tintco will rebut that Balm was an infrequently used scalp medication and Gloria's use of it with Tintco was an unforeseeable intervening act sufficient to break the chain of causation.

However, even though Balm may have been an infrequently used scalp medication, its use was known. Further, since Gloria is the plaintiff, her act of using Balm is not considered an intervening act. It was direct and foreseeable.

Tintco is the proximate cause of Gloria's damages.

General Damages

Gloria's hair turned purple from the use of Tint which caused her embarrassment during the time it took for her hair to grow out. This form of pain and suffering will be recoverable general damages.

Special Damages

As a result of her hair turning purple, Gloria will assert that she was forced to withdraw from the beauty contest for which she had been regarded as the favorite. Further, she lost any gratuities and publicity that would have been received had she won the contest and will seek recovery for these damages.

However, even though Gloria was the favorite, there was no guarantee that she would ultimately win. Thus, any claim that she was damaged when she had to withdraw from the contest was speculative since she could not show losses to any reasonable certainty of an amount.

Further, the loss of a beauty contest was not a foreseeable result of Tintco's breach making such a loss too remote.

Gloria will not be able to recover special damages.

Breach of Express Warranty

An express warranty is a promise or representation of fact made by a commercial seller to a buyer relating to the quality of good which causes reliance to one's damage.

Gloria will argue that Tintco, a commercial seller, represented its product as safe and wholesome when it used Mag's Seal of Approval in its advertising and on Tint container labels. Gloria, a buyer, reasonably relied on these representations of quality when she purchased the product and used it on her hair.

However, Tint was not safe and wholesome as advertised when used in combination with Balm. It turned her hair purple making Tint less than a quality product. Tint did not perform as expressly represented.

Tintco breached its express warranty and will be held liable for general damages as discussed supra.

Breach of Implied Warranty - Merchantability

The implied assurance from seller to consumer that the product is fair and of average quality.

Because the use of Tint in combination with Balm caused Gloria's hair to turn purple, it was not fit for normal use. Tintco's failure to warn of this side effect further made it less than fair and average quality.
Tintco will be held liable for breach of implied warranty and subject to the general damages supra.

Breach of Implied Warranty - Fitness for Intended Purpose

Where a seller knows of a purchaser's particular use of his product and that the purchaser is relying on the seller's skill in supplying appropriate goods, there is an implied warranty that the goods sold are fit for that purpose.

Tintco knew that Tint was sold as a hair coloring and would be applied for that particular purpose. Further, Gloria as a consumer and beauty contestant, relied on the skill of Tintco to produce a hair coloring that would be appropriate and fit for that purpose.

When Tint caused her hair to turn purple, she was severely damaged.

Tintco may be liable for its breach of the implied warranty of fitness for an intended purpose.

Strict Liability in Tort

If a defective product is placed in the stream of commerce, the manufacturer will beheld strictly liable in tort to all consumer-users for their injuries
(**Greenman v. Yuba Power**).

Tint was produced and sold without adequate testing and without adequate warnings regarding its use with Balm. Tintco allowed it to leave its control in this condition when it sold it to Gloria. This dangerous condition would not be expected by an ordinary consumer in normal use. Thus, Tint was unreasonably dangerous (**Restatement 2nd 402A**).

Tintco will rebut that it did not know that the contact between Tint and Balm could result in purple hair and, therefore, could not foresee any danger to consumers from the normal use of the hair color.

However, the Tint caused harm to Gloria's hair during its normal use. It failed to perform as expected when used in its intended manner. Tintco's lack of knowledge would not shield it from liability (**California Jurisdiction**).

In addition, the defect was in existence at the time it was placed in the stream of commerce making it a defective product.

Actual Causation

As discussed, supra. under Negligence.

Proximate Causation

As discussed, supra. under Negligence.

Damages

As discussed, supra. under Negligence.

Tintco will be held liable for strict liability in tort.

2. GLORIA v. MAG

Negligent Misrepresentation

Negligent misrepresentation is the misrepresentation of a material fact made with a lack of due care which induces the justifiable reliance of the plaintiff causing damages.

Mag's Seal of Approval which indicated that Tint was safe, effective and wholesome when, in fact, it caused hair to turn purple when used with Balm, was a misrepresentation of a material fact. Since Mag was unaware of this side effect at the time it authorized its Seal of Approval, the misrepresentation was made with a lack of due care.

It is reasonable to infer that the Seal of Approval may have played a substantial part in inducing Gloria to use Tint. If it did, her actual reliance on its safety and effectiveness was justifiable. Gloria's purple hair would demonstrate damages.

Mag will be liable for negligent misrepresentation.

Negligence

Negligence requires a showing that a duty was owed, that the duty was breached and the breach was the actual and proximate cause of damages.

Duty

Mag, as a magazine publisher, owed a duty of due care to operate its testing lab properly so that it could adequately determine the safety and wholesomeness of the products it advertised before authorizing its endorsement so as not to expose consumers to an unreasonable risk of harm. Since Gloria was a user of Tint on which Mag's Seal of Approval appeared, she was a foreseeable plaintiff.

Therefore, Mag owed a duty to Gloria.

Breach

Gloria will contend that despite Mag's tests, it did not discover that when Tint was used in combination with Balm, purple hair would result.

Its failure to determine this fact and to either warn or withhold its Seal of Approval fell below the standard of care required from the average reasonable manufacturer under the same or similar circumstances.

Mag breached its duty of due care.

Actual Causation

Mag's failure to adequately test and/or withhold its Seal of Approval in conjunction with Tintco's negligence (supra) was a substantial factor resulting in the damage to Gloria's hair.

Mag is actual cause of Gloria's damages.

Proximate Causation

It was foreseeable that Gloria and other consumers would rely on Mag's Seal of Approval when choosing to use Tint. It is further foreseeable that Tint would be used with other hair products as discussed supra.

Thus, Mag is the proximate cause of Gloria's hair damage.

Damages

See discussion of general damages under products liability negligence supra.

TORTS QUESTION #5

JILL v. DON

Jill, a married public school teacher in her late twenties, became involved several years ago in an affair with Don, her principal at Hudson High School. Jill broke off the relationship after counseling with her minister. Since that time Don has attempted to continue the affair. He called Jill at her home, threatened to make a full disclosure to Jill's husband, and, without cause, charged her with violation of school regulations.

Because of Don's harassment, Jill resigned her position at Hudson effective at the end of the school year and applied for a new teaching position for the next school year at Clark High School in an adjoining school district. She was notified by Clark officials that her application had been accepted and that she would be employed for the next school year. A few days later, however, she received notice from Clark that upon reconsideration her application had been "finally rejected."

Jill was advised by a Clark official that, in response to Clark's inquiry, Don had reported that Jill was a woman of poor moral character who often appeared at work with alcohol on her breath. The Clark official stated that her application had been rejected based on the information supplied by Don. In fact, Jill has never appeared at work with alcohol on her breath.

Jill commenced an action against Don seeking damages. Jill alleged that she is now unable to find employment with other schools because schools routinely make inquiry of former school employers; that she is unable to find other employment except as a waitress at two-thirds the compensation she could earn as a teacher; that she had declined such other employment; and that because of fear and emotional trauma she has suffered and is continuing to suffer embarrassment and humiliation.

What damages, if any, are Jill entitled to against Don? Discuss.

IRAC OUTLINE SHEET

(I)	(R)	(A)	(C)

EXAMPLE OF PROPER IRAC OUTLINE

JILL (J) v. DON (D)

(I)	(R)	(A)	(C)
INTENTIONAL INFLICTION OF EMOTIONAL DISTRESS	Intentional/Outrageous Conduct	D has attempted to continue affair Called J at home/threatened to make full disclosure to J's husband/without cause charged J with school regs violation	Liable
	Calculated To/Does Cause Severe Emotional Distress	Supra facts J resigned position at Hudson Fear/emotional trauma/embarrassment/ humiliation	
DEFAMATION	False Defamatory Statement	J a woman of poor moral character/ often appeared at work with alcohol on breath (false?)	Liable
	Intentional Negligent Publication 3rd Person	In response to inquiry, D reported to Clark official	
	Understood as Defamatory	Application initially accepted -- upon reconsideration, finally rejected	
	Causation	D's statements resulted in loss of job	
	Damages (Slander Per Se)	Married public school teacher/poor moral character (chastity) Alcohol on breath at work/never at work with alcohol on breath (business)	
DEFENSE – TRUTH	Complete Defense	J became involved in affair with D J broke off affair after counseling with minister Alcohol – never appeared at work with alcohol on breath	No Defense
QUALIFIED PRIVILEGE	Legitimate Interest of Others	In response to Clark's inquiry, D reported supra D has attempted to continue the affair	No Privilege
INVASION OF PRIVACY	Intrusion Upon Seclusion	D called J at home/threatened full disclosure to husband	Liable
	Expectation of Privacy	D called J at home	
INTERFERENCE WITH CONTRACT	Intentional Interference	D's harassment/threats	Liable
	Existing Contrast	J resigned position at Hudson effective at end of school year	
	Damages	Loss of wages	
INTERFERENCE WITH PROSPECTIVE ADVANTAGE	Intentional Interference	D reported to Clark supra J's application accepted/finally rejected	Liable
	Prospective Advantage	J applied for teaching position at Clark Notified application accepted	
	Damages	Loss of job	

(I)	(R)	(A)	(C)
TRADE LIBEL	False Statement	See defamation facts	Liable
	Intent to Disparage Business	Poor moral character Alcohol on breath at work/D a school Principal	
	Publication	Supra	
	Special Damages	Application rejected – lost wages (Economic)	
GENERAL DAMAGES	Present	Fear/emotional trauma/embarrassment/ humiliation – (pain & suffering)	General Damages
SPECIAL DAMAGES	Reasonable Certainty Of Money Amount	Salary loss (Economic Losses)	Special Damages
	Proximate Cause	Unable to find employment with other school because of routine inquiry of former school employers	
	Not Too Remote	Unable to find other employment other than waitress at 2/3 compensation which J declined	
PUNITIVE DAMAGES	Willful/Malicious	Harassment/D's reports supra	Punitive Damages

EXAMPLE OF IRAC TORTS ISSUE

(I) **Defamation**

(R) Defamation is (1) a false defamatory statement (2) intentionally or negligently published to a third party which is (3) understood as defamatory by that third party (4) causing (5) damages to plaintiff's reputation.

(A) Jill will assert that Don's reported statements that she was a woman of poor moral character who often appeared at work with alcohol on her breath were (1) false and would tend to lower her reputation in the teaching community making it defamatory in nature.

Don's statements were made to a Clark School official in response to his employment inquiry and were, thus, (2) an intentional publication to a third person.

Even though Jill's employment application had been initially accepted, Don's report to the Clark official instigated the reconsideration of her application which demonstrates that the official reasonably perceived Don's report as a statement of fact. She was then "finally rejected" indicating that such statements were, in fact, (3) understood as defamatory.

"But for" Don's statements, Jill would have been hired. Further, his report caused her application to be rejected which was the foreseeable result of his statements. Don was the (4) cause of her loss.

The statement concerning her moral character damaged her reputation as a chaste married school teacher. The statement concerning alcohol on her breath at work damaged her business reputation. As such, Don's statements will constitute slander per se and Jill may recover (5) general damages without first proving special damages.

(C) Don will be liable for defamation.

SUGGESTED MODEL ANSWER

JILL v. DON

Intentional Infliction of Emotional Distress

Intentional infliction of emotional distress is the intentional outrageous conduct by the defendant which is calculated to cause and which does cause severe emotional distress.

Jill will contend that Don's act of calling her at home to threaten full disclosure of their past affair to her husband if she didn't continue the affair, and his charging her with school regulation violations without cause was intentional and outrageous conduct calculated to cause her emotional anguish.

His harassment did, in fact, cause her resignation at the school where they both worked. The fear, emotional trauma, embarrassment and humiliation created by Don was more than a reasonable person could be expected to endure. Such mental anguish equated to severe emotional distress.

Don will be liable to Jill for intentional infliction of emotional distress.

Defamation

Defamation is a false defamatory statement intentionally or negligently published to a third party, which is understood as defamatory by that third party causing damages to plaintiff's reputation.

Jill will assert that Don's reported statements that she was a woman of poor moral character who often appeared at work with alcohol on her breath were false and would tend to lower her reputation in the teaching community making it defamatory in nature.

Don's statements were made to a Clark School official in response to his employment inquiry and was, thus, an intentional publication to a third person.

Even though Jill's employment application had been initially accepted, Don's report to the Clark official instigated the reconsideration of her application which demonstrates that the official reasonably perceived Don's report as a statement of fact. She was then "finally rejected" indicating that such statements were, in fact, understood as defamatory.

"But for" Don's statements, Jill would have been hired. Further, his report caused her application to be rejected which was the foreseeable result of his statements. Don was the cause of her loss.

The statement concerning her moral character damaged her reputation as a chaste married school teacher. The statement concerning alcohol on her breath at work damaged her business reputation. As such, Don's statements will constitute slander per se and Jill may recover general damages without first proving special damages.

Don will be liable for defamation.

Defense - Truth

Truth of a defamatory matter is a complete defense.

Don will argue that Jill was a married woman at the time that they were having an affair. Therefore, his report that she was a woman of poor moral character was true, giving him a complete defense.

However, a single affair does not necessarily mean that Jill was a woman of poor moral character. In fact, she broke off the affair subsequent to counseling with her minister which indicates that she wanted to preserve her moral character. Further, the statement concerning alcohol on her breath was completely false since she had never appeared at work in this condition.

Truth will not be valid defense.

Qualified Privilege

A person has a qualified privilege to defame another if he reasonably believes his statements are necessary to protect a legitimate public interest and that the person to whom the statement is made has the power to protect that interest.

Don's statements were made in response to an employment inquiry from Jill's prospective employer. He reasonably believed that he must disclose his knowledge of Jill's character to protect the legitimate public interest for qualified teachers. The Clark official to whom he spoke had the power to consider this information when deciding whether Jill was a qualified candidate for the job.

However, it appears that Don's statements were motivated by his desire to harass Jill when his attempts to continue the affair were rebuffed. He was not acting out of a desire to protect the public interest for qualified teachers. Rather, he was acting out of malice and an intent to injure Jill. Thus, any qualified privilege he may have had to report Jill's work habits was lost through his abuse.

The qualified privilege will not apply.

Invasion of Privacy

Invasion of privacy involves the right to be let alone. One theory of recovery is the intentional intrusion into the seclusion of a person where there is a reasonable expectation of privacy.

Don called Jill at home to threaten full disclosure of their affair to her husband which was a volitional and intentional intrusion into the seclusion of her home. Since she had a reasonable expectation of privacy there, Don will be liable for invasion of privacy.

Interference With Contract

Interference with contract is the intentional interference with an existing contract which causes damage.

Don's harassment and threats were volitional acts. They were calculated to intentionally interfere with her responsibilities as a school teacher at Hudson High. As a result, her performance became so difficult that she was forced to resign the position under her existing teaching contract at Hudson at the end of the school year.

Her resignation undoubtedly resulted in loss of wages sufficient to demonstrate damages.

Don will be liable for intentional interference with contract.

Interference With a Prospective Advantage

The intentional interference with a prospective advantage.

When Don reported the defamatory statements to the Clark official (supra) he intended to interfere with Jill's prospective employment advantage as a teacher at that school. In fact, his statements did cause an interference since her application which had previously been accepted was "finally rejected" following that conversation. Such rejection resulted in a loss of the job sufficient to demonstrate damages.

Don will be liable for intentional interference with a prospective advantage.

Trade Libel

Trade Libel is a false statement, made by a defendant with the intent to disparage the plaintiff's business which is published to a third party causing special damages.

As previously discussed, Don's statements regarding Jill's moral character and alcohol use at work were false. As a school principal, Don knew that such information would be reasonably likely to discourage Clark High from hiring Jill to teach its students. Don's report demonstrates his intent to disparage Jill's business as a teacher.

The fact that Don reported these statements to the Clark official demonstrates publication. Since Don's statements were the cause of her application rejection, Jill can show the loss of wages as special damages.

Don will be liable for trade libel.

Remedy - Damages

Generals

General damages are present damages such as the law itself implies or presumes to have accrued from the wrong complained of.

Jill will seek compensation for the fear, emotional trauma, embarrassment and humiliation which are forms of pain and suffering that the law presumes to have accrued from the torts committed by Don.

General damages will be awarded.

Special Damages

Special damages involve all economic losses and expenses the plaintiff has suffered as a result of the injury. There must be a reasonable certainly of money amount, a proximate cause relationship to the wrong, which is not too remote in nature.

Jill will establish that she was forced to resign from Hudson High, her application at Clark was rejected, and she was unable to find other teaching employment. These employment and wage losses were the actual result of Don's torts (supra). The amount of these salary losses can be calculated to a reasonable certainty. Since they were the proximate consequence of Don's torts, they are foreseeable and not too remote.

Don will counter that Jill had a duty to mitigate the amount of her salary losses by accepting the waitress position that was available and paid 2/3 the amount of her teaching salary. Her decline of such employment was an unjustified refusal to mitigate her losses.

However, Jill was not legally bound to accept employment outside of her profession to reduce her damages he benefit of the defendant. She is entitled to employment in her stated profession and the defendant will remain liable for the loss of wages associated with that profession.

Special damages will be awarded.

Punitive Damages

Punitive damages are those damages awarded to the plaintiff where the wrong complained of was aggravated by willful, wanton acts of the defendant.

Jill will argue that Don's harassment, threats and wanton conduct regarding her morals and alcohol use (supra) justifies an award of punitive damages to punish him for his vindictive conduct.

Punitive damages will be awarded.

SECTION VI

CONTRACTS

CONTRACTS

LEARN TO WRITE THE RIGHT WAY®

CONTRACTS QUESTION #1

YELLOWHOUSE/GREENHOUSE

On Monday, February 1, Bob received the following letter from Alex: "Dear Bob, I will let you have my "Oceanhaven" home for this May through June season, same terms under which you occupied it last year. Please reply in a week."

Earlier in January, Bob had made an inquiry at "The Shores", an ocean resort owned by Tom. In Tom's absence, Dave, one of Tom's caretakers, had shown Bob two available houses, "Yellowhouse" and "Greenhouse", owned by Tom, which Dave stated were listed to rent at $5,000 and $2,000 respectively, for one season.

On February 2, Bob received a letter from Tom which read, "This confirms all statements by Dave. You may have "Yellowhouse" at $5,000, or "Greenhouse" at $2,000, for the May through June season, all services included, payable in equal monthly installments."

On February 4, Bob wrote to Tom as follows, "I believe your prices are high. Will you take $4,000 for "Yellowhouse"? If not, then I'll have to settle for "Greenhouse," and I agree to the $2,000 you ask, only I hope you will drop the price if I pay the whole $2,000 in advance."

On February 4, Bob learned from his real estate agent that Alex had leased "Oceanhaven" to Smith for 6 months effective March 1.

On February 5, Tom received Bob's letter and Tom immediately telegraphed Bob, "No change in prices. See my letter of February 2." Bob received Tom's telegram the same day, February 5; and later that day also received Tom's letter of February 5th, which read, "Our deal is off." Bob immediately wrote Alex, "I'll take "Oceanhaven" per your letter of February 1."

Bob sues Alex as well as Tom, discuss all contractual rights involved.

IRAC OUTLINE SHEET

(I)	(R)	(A)	(C)

EXAMPLE OF PROPER IRAC OUTLINE

BOB v. ALEX

(I)	(R)	(A)	(C)
OFFER	Intent	2/1 letter "I'll let you have"	Offer
	Definite/Certain Terms	One rental (quantity) May-June (time) B/A (parties) Same term as last year (price?) Oceanhaven (subject matter)	
	Communicated to Offeree	Letter sent/received Reply in one week	
INDIRECT REVOCATION	Reliable Source	B learned from his real estate agent	Indirect Revocation
	Acts Inconsistent	Oceanhaven leased Smith for 6 months effective 3/1. B's K May – June	
ACCEPTANCE	Unequivocal Assent	2/5 letter "I'll take Oceanhaven per 2/1 letter:"	Acceptance
	Terms of Offer	B sent reply in one week (timely?) Effect of 2/4 indirect revocation	

BOB v. TOM

(I)	(R)	(A)	(C)
OFFER	Intent	Negotiations with Dave (preliminary?) 2/2 letter "This confirms all statements by Dave, you may have"	Offer
	Definite/Certain Terms	Two rentals (quantity) May-June (time) B&T (parties) $5,000 for Yellowhouse (price) $2,000 Greenhouse (price) Yellowhouse/Greenhouse rentals (subject matter)	
	Communicated To Offeree	Letter sent & received	
COUNTER OFFER (YELLOWHOUSE)	Words/Conduct	2/4 letter to T – "I believe your prices are high will you take $4,000 for Yellowhouse?"	Counter Offer
	Understood as Rejection	"No change in prices"	
ACCEPTANCE (GREENHOUSE)	Unequivocal Assent	2/4 letter to T – "If not, I'll have to settle for Greenhouse. I agree to the $2,000 you ask" "Only hope you drop the price if I pay whole $2,000 in advance	Acceptance
	Terms of Offer	2/4 offer still open	
REVOCATION	Express Language	"Deal off"	Revocation
	Prior To Timely Acceptance	2/5 revocation/received on 2/5 2/4 acceptance – supra	
CONSIDERATION	Bargained for Exchange (Benefit/Detriment)	$2,000 for rental of Greenhouse	Consideration

EXAMPLE OF IRAC CONTRACTS ISSUE

(I) **Indirect Revocation**

(R) (1) Knowledge by an offeree from a reliable source that the offeror cannot perform requires (2) acts inconsistent with the contract.

(A) Alex will argue that when Bob learned from his own real estate agent that Oceanhaven had been leased to Smith, his (1) knowledge of the unavailability of Oceanhaven came from a person charged with the responsibility to provide Bob with correct information and was, thus, from a reliable source.

Further, Bob was told that Smith's lease agreement for Oceanhaven was effective on March 1st for a period of six months. Since Smith's lease would not expire until August, Alex's (2) act of leasing to Smith during this time was inconsistent with his ability to contract with Bob from May through June.

(C) Therefore, Smith's lease would constitute a valid indirect revocation.

SUGGESTED MODEL ANSWER

BOB v. ALEX

Offer

An offer is an outward manifestation of intent to be bound by contractual agreement requiring definite and certain terms communicated to the offeree.

Bob will contend that Alex's letter dated February 1st clearly stated, "I will let you have my Oceanhaven home," which was language indicating his outward manifestation of intent to be bound to a rental agreement. The terms were stated as quantity -- one rental, time -- May through June, identity of parties -- Bob and Alex, price – "same terms as you occupied last year" which could be reasonably implied as the price paid a year earlier, and subject matter -- Oceanhaven. Since these terms were mentioned with particularity, they were definite and certain.

The letter contained a request for a one week reply. It was sent to and received by Bob, which constitutes communication to the offeree.

Therefore, Alex's February 1st letter was a valid offer.

Indirect Revocation

Knowledge by an offeree from a reliable source that the offeror cannot perform requires acts inconsistent with the contract.

Alex will argue that when Bob learned from his own real estate agent that Oceanhaven had been leased to Smith, his knowledge of the unavailability of Oceanhaven came from a person charged with the responsibility to provide Bob with correct information and was, thus, from a reliable source.

Further, Bob was told that Smith's lease agreement for Oceanhaven was effective on March 1st for a period of six months. Since Smith's lease would not expire until August, Alex's act of leasing to Smith during this time was inconsistent with his ability to contract with Bob from May through June.

Therefore, Smith's lease would constitute a valid indirect revocation.

Acceptance

Acceptance is an unequivocal assent to the terms of the offer.

When Bob wrote to Alex on February 5th and stated, "I'll take Oceanhaven per your February 1st letter," his language was an unequivocal assent to the terms of the offer. Further, Bob's letter was sent within the week that Alex had given him to reply making his assent timely.

However, Bob's letter was not sent until after the February 4th indirect revocation (supra). The offer had, thus, expired because Alex's allowance for a one week reply was gratuitous and not binding. Bob's attempted assent was not timely.

Therefore, due to a lack of mutual assent, Bob has no contractual right to Oceanhaven.

BOB v. TOM

Offer

Defined supra.

Bob will assert that he initially entered into preliminary negotiations with Tom's caretaker, Dave, when he made an inquiry as to the availability of the Shores ocean rentals. However, when Tom wrote to Bob on February 2nd and stated, "This confirms all statements by Dave, you may have...," Tom's language demonstrated an outward manifestation of his intent to be bound to a rental agreement.

The terms were stated as quantity -- two rental houses, time - listed to rent May through June, identity of parties -- Tom and Bob, price -- $5,000 for Yellowhouse and $2,000 for Green-house, subject matter -- ocean resort rentals. Because these terms were stated with particularity, they were definite and certain.

Since the letter was sent to and received by Bob, it was communicated to the offeree.

Therefore, a valid offer exists.

Counter Offer - Yellowhouse

Words or conduct which a reasonable person would understand as a rejection of an offer, is a counter offer.

Tom will assert that Bob's February 4th letter containing the words, "I believe your prices are high. Will you take $4,000 for Yellowhouse?", would lead a reasonable person to understand that Bob would not pay the quoted price of $5,000. Bob was instead attempting to change the price term to $4,000.
Tom's reply, "there would be no change in prices," demonstrated his understanding that Bob's attempt to lower the price to $4,000 was a rejection of the offer for Yellowhouse at the $5,000 price.

Further, since Tom did not accept Bob's $4,000 offer no mutual assent exists as to Yellowhouse.

Therefore, Bob's February 4th letter acted as a valid counter offer.

Acceptance - Greenhouse

Defined supra.

Bob will contend that even though he grumbled about the price of Greenhouse in his February 4th letter when he wrote, "If not, I'll have to settle" and "I only hope you drop the price if I pay the whole $2,000 in advance, he was only expressing a wish for a reduced price, not a condition that he would not take it otherwise. Further, his language stating "I agree to the $2,000 you ask," demonstrated his intent to rent Greenhouse for the $2,000 price and was, thus, and unequivocal assent to the terms of the offer.

Bob sent his letter on February 4th at a time when Tom's offer was still open. Thus, under the **Adams v. Lindsell** mailbox rule, his acceptance was effective upon dispatch.

Therefore, Bob's February 4th letter was a valid acceptance of Greenhouse.

Revocation

An offeror may expressly revoke an offer as long as it is communicated to the offeree prior to a timely acceptance. It is effective upon receipt.

Tom will assert that on February 5th, he wrote to Bob and stated "The deal is off" which was express language showing his clear intent to revoke the offer on Greenhouse.

However, Tom's revocation was sent to and received by Bob February 5th after Bob had already sent Tom his February 4th acceptance (supra).

Therefore, it was not communicated prior to timely acceptance.

Tom's February 5th letter is an invalid revocation.

Consideration

Consideration is that which is bargained for and given in exchange for a return promise requiring benefit or detriment.

Bob will argue that his promise to pay $2,000 for Greenhouse was bargained for and given in exchange for Tom's return promise to rent Greenhouse to him. Bob incurred the detriment of having to pay the $2,000 for the rental and received the benefit of an ocean resort rental. Tom incurred the detriment of having to rent to Bob for $2,000 and received the benefit of a $2,000 rental.

Since valid consideration exists, Bob has a valid contractual right to the rental of Greenhouse.

CONTRACTS QUESTION #2

MOTORS v. JONES

On January 15, 1983, Jones agreed with Motors in a writing signed by both to supply Motors with 10,000 pounds of specifically described bolts each month, for a period of ten months, beginning March 1, 1983. The stated price was $.85 per pound. On February 1, 1983, Jones, in good faith, notified Motors that he could not afford to sell the bolts at the agreed price. He said he would charge $.90 per pound. Motors orally agreed to the increase in price to begin with the first installment.

In a written confirmation, signed only by Jones and delivered to Motors, Jones' secretary mistakenly typed the new price as "$.91 per pound" rather than "$.90 per pound." Motors received the confirmation but did not read it and did not reply to it.

Prior to March 1, 1983, Jones notified Motors that he would deliver no bolts because he had just contracted to sell his entire output to Ted at $1.10 per pound.

Despite diligent efforts, Motors was unable to buy bolts from a new supplier until May 1. The price charged by the new supplier was $1.00 per pound

Because of the 60 day delay in obtaining a new source of supply, Motors was delayed in delivering motors to Electric, a company with which Motors had a contract that contained a valid liquidated damages clause providing for damages of $10,000 a day for delay in delivery of motors.

Although Jones knew that Motors sold motors, he did not know specifically nor did he have reason to know, that Motors had a contract with Electric or that that contract contained a liquidated damages clause.

In a suit by Motors against Jones commenced on October 1, 1983, Motors prays for the following damages.

> Count 1: $15,000, being the difference between the price paid by Motors ($1.00) and the original contract price ($.85) for 100,000 pounds;
>
> Count 2: $600,000, being the amount Motors had to pay Electric in liquidated damages;
>
> Count 3: $1,000,000 as punitive damages, alleging that Jones' breach was malicious.

In his answer to the complaint, Jones denies liability for damages, and contends that if he should be found liable under count 1, his liability would be limited to $9,000, being the difference between the price paid by Motors ($1.00) and the modified price in the written confirmation ($.91).

What result on each count, and what amount of damages, if any, should be awarded? Discuss.

IRAC OUTLINE SHEET

(I)	(R)	(A)	(C)

EXAMPLE OF PROPER IRAC OUTLINE

MOTORS v. JONES

(I)	(R)	(A)	(C)
U.C.C.	Sale of Goods	Specifically described bolts	U.C.C. Applies
MERCHANT	Deals in Kind of Goods Involved	J agreed to supply 10,000 bolts per month for 10 months	Merchant
OFFER	Intent	J agreed in writing 1/15/83 to supply 10,000 lbs. specifically described bolts to M per month	
	Definite/Certain Terms	10,000 bolts (quantity) Each month for ten months beginning 3/1/83 (time) J/M (parties) .85 per lb. (price) Specifically described bolts (subject matter)	Offer
	Communicated to Offeree	J/M agreed in writing/signed	
ACCEPTANCE	Unequivocal Assent	J/M agreed in writing/signed	Acceptance
	Term s of Offer	J/M agreed in writing/signed	
CONSIDERATION	Bargained for Exchange (Benefit/Detriment)	Bolts for money Sell 10,000 lbs. bolts for 10 months at .85 per lb. 2/1/83 J, in good faith, notified M	Consideration
MODIFICATION-COMMON LAW	Change in Terms	Couldn't afford to sell at agreed price/would charge .90 per lb.	No Common Law Consideration
	Mutual Assent	M orally agreed to increase Price of .85 per lb. already agreed	
	Consideration	Price of .85 under original OFFER supra (pre-existing duty)	
MODIFICATION--U.C.C.	Merchant Agreement	2/1/83 agreement supra	Valid U.C.C. Modification
	Good Faith	J, in good faith, couldn't afford to sell at .85 per lb.	
DEFENSE--STATUTE OF FRAUDS	Written Contract for Goods Over $500.00	Written contract supra 2/1/83 modification	Valid Defense
	Oral Modification	10,000 bolts per month at .90 per lb.	
	Writing	Oral	
EXCEPTION-SUFFICIENT MEMO COMMON LAW	Memo with Essential Terms	J sent written, signed confirmation of price change	Invalid Exception
	Signed by Party Charged	Written confirmation delivered to M/ did not read or reply	
EXCEPTION-WRITTEN CONFIRMATION--U.C.C.	Merchant Written Confirmation	J sent written confirmation of price Change	Valid Exception
	Another Merchant	Motor supra	
	Bound Unless Objects in 10 Days	Written confirmation delivered to M Did not read reply	
MISTAKE-SCRIVENOR'S ERROR	Oral Agreement Mistranscribed	In written confirmation, J's secretary mistakenly typed .91 per lb. Rather than .90 per lb./M did not read or reply	Mistake
	Reformation Remedy	.90 per lb. As per modification	

(I)	(R)	(A)	(C)
CONDITION	Happening/Non-Happening Event Creates Duty To Perform	Delivery of 10,000 lbs. bolts per mo. J to supply M with 10,000 lbs. bolt for 10 months/M to pay .90 per lb. (Condition precedent?)	Condition
ANTICIPATORY REPUDIATION	Unequivocal Repudiation	Supply of bolts to begin 3/1/83 Prior to 3/1/83, J notified M that he would deliver no bolts because he had contracted to sell entire output to T for $1.10 per lb.	Anticipatory Repudiation
VOLUNTARY DISABLEMENT	Repudiation Through Conduct	J notified M that he contracted to sell entire output to T (supra,	Voluntary Disablement
BREACH	Unjustified Failure To Perform	J notified M that he contracted to sell entire output to T (supra)	Breach
	Essence of Bargain	Bolts	
GENERAL DAMAGES	Expectancy Under Contract	.90 per lb. see modification	General Damages
	Cover-U.C.C.	Despite diligent efforts, unable to buy from new supplier until 5/1/83 at $1.00 per lbs.	
SPECIAL DAMAGES	Foreseeable/Natural Result	Although J knew that M sold motors, he did not know specifically or have reason to know of its contract with E of liquidated damages clause	No Special Damages
PUNITIVE DAMAGES	Willful/Malicious	M alleges breach malicious/no facts to support	No Punitive Damages

EXAMPLE OF IRAC CONTRACTS ISSUE

(I) **Offer**

(R) An offer is (1) an outward manifestation of intent to be bound by contractual agreement requiring (2) definite and certain terms (3) communicated to the offeree.

(A) When Jones agreed in writing on January 15, 1983 to supply Motors with 10,000 lbs. of specifically described bolts, the language of the agreement demonstrated (1) his outward manifestation of present intent to be contractually bound.

The terms were described as quantity, 10,000 bolts -- time, ten months beginning March 1, 1983 -- identity of parties, Jones/Motors -- price .85/lb. -- subject matter, specifically described bolts. Since the (2) terms were mentioned with particularity, they were definite and certain under the common law. Under U.C.C., the only term required is quantity which has also been satisfied.

The agreement was in the form of a signed writing by both Jones and Motors which demonstrated (3) communication to the offeree.

(C) The agreement constituted a valid offer.

SUGGESTED MODEL ANSWER

MOTORS v. JONES

U.C.C.

Contracts for the sale of goods are governed by the rules of U.C.C.

Since the Motors/Jones transaction dealt with specifically described bolts, those items would qualify as a sale of goods under the U.C.C.

Merchants

A merchant is a person who deals in the kind of goods involved in the transaction or otherwise holds himself out as having knowledge or skill peculiar to the practices or goods involved in the transaction.

Jones was dealing in the sale of large quantities of bolts for what appears to be a long period of time. He transacted to supply Motors with the 10,000 pounds of specifically described bolts for ten months and, thus, held himself out as having the knowledge and skill peculiar to completing the order.

Motors was buying these bolts for its business and, thus, also dealt in the kind of goods involved in the transaction.

Thus, both parties would be considered merchants under the U.C.C.

Validity of Contract - Offer

An offer is an outward manifestation of intent to be bound by contractual agreement requiring definite and certain terms communicated to the offeree.

When Jones agreed in writing on January 15, 1983 to supply Motors with 10,000 lbs. of specifically described bolts, the language of the agreement demonstrated his outward manifestation of present intent to be contractually bound.

The terms were described as quantity, 10,000 bolts -- time, ten months beginning March 1, 1983 -- identity of parties, Jones/Motors -- price, .85/lb. -- subject matter, specifically described bolts. Since the terms were mentioned with particularity , they were definite and certain under the common law. Under U.C.C., the only term required is quantity which has also been satisfied.

The agreement was in the form of a signed writing by both Jones and Motors which demonstrated communication to the offeree.

The agreement constituted a valid offer.

Acceptance

Acceptance is an unequivocal assent to the terms of the offer.

Because both parties signed the agreement, Motors unequivocally assented to the terms of the offer. Thus, valid acceptance existed.

Consideration

Consideration is that which is bargained for and given in exchange for a return promise requiring benefit or detriment.

Here, Jones bargained for money in exchange for a return promise from Motors to buy bolts. Further, Jones obligated himself to sell Motors 10,000 bolts per month for ten months which he was not previously obligated to do. This was a detriment incurred in exchange for the benefit he would receive from the $.85 per lb. derived from the sale.

Motors obligated itself to buy the bolts which it was not previously obligated to do. This was a detriment incurred for the exchange benefit of having its needs for bolts satisfied.

Therefore, since, consideration is present a valid contract was formed.

Modification - Common Law

A modification is a change in the terms of the original offer requiring mutual assent and consideration.

When Jones contacted Motors on February 1, 1983 and notified it that he could not afford to sell the bolts for $.85 per lb., saying instead that he would charge $.90 per lb., he was attempting to change the price term of the original offer. Motors' oral agreement to the price increase beginning with the first installment demonstrated an acceptance sufficient for mutual assent.

However, Jones was under a pre-existing duty to supply Motors with the bolts at the original contracting price (supra). By increasing the price without obligating himself to any new detriment that he was not previously obligated to, there was no bargained for exchange. Thus, there was no consideration.

The modification will fail under common law.

Modification - U.C.C.

An agreement between merchants modifying a contract for the sale of goods needs no consideration if it is made in good faith.

As discussed supra, Motors and Jones were merchants. The agreement to change the price of the bolts involved the sale of goods. When Jones found that he could not afford to sell the bolts for $.85 per lb., he made a good faith effort to establish a new price that was fair and equitable in order to supply Motors as agreed. In view of the fact that the necessity for a price increase was not anticipated when the contract was originally formed, consideration for the new price term will not be required.

The modification will be valid under the U.C.C.

Defense - Statute of Frauds

A written contract for the sale of goods for $500 or more that is orally modified must be in writing.

The contract involved the sale of bolts in excess of $500. Since the modification was oral, it would be barred by the Statute of Frauds for lack of a writing.

The Statute of Frauds is a valid defense.

Exception - Sufficient Memorandum

A memorandum of the essential terms of the agreement will satisfy the Statute of Frauds if it is signed by the party to be charged.

Jones will assert that he sent a written confirmation of the agreement which was delivered to Motors. It contained the essential terms concerning the change in price and was signed by Jones. This constituted a sufficient writing.

However, although Motors received the confirmation, it did not read it, reply to it or sign it. Thus, it was not signed by the party to be charged. The fact that Jones, as the party seeking to enforce the contract, has signed the confirmation is immaterial.

This exception will be invalid.

Exception - Written Confirmation - U.C.C.

The U.C.C. provides that if a merchant sends a written confirmation of a contract to another, the other merchant is bound and is held to have signed unless he objects within ten days following receipt of the confirmation.

Jones sent a written confirmation to Motors which memorialized the change in price.

As such, when Motors received the confirmation, it was charged with the responsibility of a merchant to either object to its contents within ten days or be bound. The fact that Motors did not read the confirmation or reply to it will not excuse it from its obligation. He is held to have signed absent an objection within ten days following receipt.

The written confirmation will act as a valid exception to the Statute of Frauds.

Mistake - Scrivenor's Error

Where the parties make an oral agreement which, when reduced to a writing, is mistranscribed, the aggrieved party is entitled to reformation so that the writing corresponds to the oral agreement.

When the written confirmation embodying the oral agreement to change the price to $.90 per lb. was sent, Jones' secretary mistakenly typed the new price $.91 per lb. Motors did not read or reply to it after it had been received and had no reason to know of the mistake. Since Jones and Motors orally agreed to the $.90 per lb. price and it was only due to the secretarial mistake that it was typed as $.91 per lb., both parties' testimony would be clear and convincing evidence that the parties' true intent was $.90 per lb.

The contract will be reformed to reflect the $.90 per lb. price.

Condition

A condition is a fact or event, the happening or non-happening of which either creates or extinguishes absolute duty to perform.

Motors will argue that Jones' delivery of 10,000 lbs. of bolts per month was the event that must happen to create its absolute duty to pay $.90 per lb.

Since, Jones' delivery must occur before Motors' duty to pay arose, Jones' delivery was a condition precedent.

Excuse - Anticipatory Repudiation

An unequivocal expression repudiating the intent to perform a contract in its executory stage.

Performance was to begin on March 1, 1983. Prior to that date, Jones notified Motors that he would deliver no bolts because he had just contracted to sell his entire output to Ted for $1.10 per lb. This language was an unequivocal expression of Jones' intent to repudiate his obligation to perform under the Jones/Motors contract. Since it took place in the executory stage of the contract, it would constitute an anticipatory repudiation.

At common law, Motors, as the innocent party, could bring an immediate action for the value of the performance.

Under the U.C.C., Motors has the right to demand adequate assurances of performance that Jones would perform as promised. Since Jones clearly stated that he intended to sell to Ted, it is doubtful that any demands by Motors would be satisfied.

Therefore, Jones' anticipatory reputation would excuse Motors condition precedent to pay.

Voluntary Disablement

Voluntary Disablement is an anticipatory repudiation through conduct.

When Jones notified Motors that he would not deliver bolts because he had contracted to sell the entire output to Ted, his conduct of obligating himself to another in a manner inconsistent with his contractual obligation to Motors was a repudiation of the Jones/Motors contract. This occurred at the executory stage of the contract and would constitute a voluntary disablement.

Thus, such would excuse Motors' duty to pay Jones under the contract.

Breach

A breach is an unjustified failure to perform which goes to the essence of the bargain.

Since Jones did not deliver the bolts to Motors because he subsequently contracted with Ted his failure to perform to Motors was unjustified.

The bolts were the basis of the contract. Because the failure to perform went to the essence of the bargain, it was a major breach.

Remedies - General Damages for Count 1

Breach of contract entitles the non-breaching party to his/ her expectancy under the contract. Under the U.C.C., a merchant is required to cover his damages.

Motors made diligent efforts to buy bolts from other suppliers in an effort to minimize the extent of his losses. He was unable to do so until May 1, two months after delivery was to have begun by Jones. He was forced to pay $1.00 per lb. instead of the $.90 per lb. originally agreed upon between Jones and Motors.

Therefore, this price was, commercially reasonable under the circumstances. He would be able to collect the difference between the modified contract price and the price of the substitute goods which would be $.10 per lb. rather than the $.15 per lb. asked for in his answer to the complaint.

Special Damages for Count 2

Special Damages are those damages that are foreseeable at time of contract and a probable result of the breach or those that naturally flow from the breach (**Hadley v. Baxendale**).

Although Jones knew at the time of contract that Motors "sold motors", he did not know specifically or have reason to know that Motors' contract with Electric contained a liquidated damages clause in the amount of $10,000 per day. Thus, these damages were not a foreseeable and probable result of the breach. A delay might foreseeably cause some loss to Motors, but a loss in the form of liquidated damages would not naturally flow from the breach.

Motors could not collect the $600,000 from Jones as special damages.

Punitive Damages for Count 3

Punitive damages are generally not recoverable for breach of contract.

Although Jones' refusal to perform was a willful bad faith breach, such conduct would not permit a recovery of punitive damages.

Therefore, Motors' prayer for $1,000,000 in punitive damages will not be recoverable.

CONTRACTS QUESTION #3

BROWNS v. MOUNTAIN PINES

In January, 1977, Mr. and Mrs. Brown learned of a rustic, but very popular, summer lodge called Mountain Pines, located in a remote section of wilderness in the mountains of a distant state. Mr. Brown wrote to Mountain Pines, describing both himself and Mrs. Brown as "city folks" who had never before been in the woods and requesting a reservation for a double room for June 1-8, of the following year, 1978. He enclosed a $100 check as a deposit.

Mountain Pines confirmed the room reservation with an unsigned postal card bearing its name in print, stated a total price of $500 and acknowledged receipt of the deposit.

The Browns arrived at the lodge in the early afternoon of June 1, 1978, only to be informed by the apologetic manager that he could not honor their reservations because all rooms would be occupied until the following evening. The manager suggested as an alternative arrangement that the Browns could stay overnight in a tent in a forested area adjacent to the lodge for only a third of the price of the room. The Browns reluctantly agreed, saying that they would do it only because they had no other choice. They paid the cost of the tent accommodations.

During the night a bear entered the tent and attacked the Browns. They suffered severe injuries, requiring $10,000 in medical expenditures. The Browns also lost $2,000 in income and incurred $1,000 additional travel expenses from Mountain Pines back to their home. The manager knew when he rented the tent to the Browns that a bear had attacked a guest in a tent at Mountain Pines during the summer of 1977.

What claims for relief may Mr. and Mrs. Brown assert against Mountain Pines? What damages will they recover if they prevail? Discuss.

IRAC OUTLINE SHEET

(I)	(R)	(A)	(C)

EXAMPLE OF PROPER IRAC OUTLINE

BROWNS v. MOUNTAIN PINES

(I)	(R)	(A)	(C)
CONTRACT LIABILITY			
OFFER	Intent	B learned of popular summer lodge B wrote to MP describing self as "city folk"/ requesting reservaton	Offer
	Definite/Certain Terms	One reservation (quantity) June 1-8. 1978 (time) B/MP (parties) Popular summer resort/$100 deposit (price?)	
	Communicated to Offeree	Reservation (subject matter)	
ACCEPTANCE	Unequivocal Assent	MP confirm room reservation/ acknowledged receipt of deposit	Acceptance
	Terms of Offer	Stated total price of $500	
CONSIDERATION	Bargained for Exchange (Benefit/Detriment)	$500/room reservation	Consideration
MODIFICATION	Change in Terms	B arrived at MP on 6/1/78 Informed reservation could not be honored Manager suggested alternative arrangement for B to stay in tent for 1/3 price	Invalid Modification
	Mutual Assent	B reluctantly agreed No other choice/city folk in remote section of wilderness	
	Consideration	1/3 price of room B paid for tent (pre-existing duty to provide room?)	Invalid Waiver
WAIVER	Voluntary Relinquishment Known Right	B reluctantly agreed to stay in tent/ no other choice	
		Confirmed room	
STATUTE OF FRAUDS	Contract Can't Be Performed In One Year	B wrote 1/77 for room 6/78	Valid Defense
EXCEPTION-SUFFICIENT MEMO	Memo	Letter/Postcard	Valid Exception
	Essential Terms	Confirmed reservation $500 total price	
	Signed	Unsigned postal card bearing name in print	
BREACH	Unjustified Failure to Performed	Reservation not honored	Breach
DAMAGES	Essence of Bargain	Tent for one night City folk/never in wilderness	
	Expectancy Under K	$100 deposit Travel expenses (Specials)	
TORT LIABILITY			
RESPONDEAT SUPERIOR	Employer/Employee	Manager of MP	Respondeat Superior
	Course/Scope Employment	Manager suggested tent/knew of prior bear attack/B city folk	

(I)	(R)	(A)	(C)
NEGLIGENCE	Duty (Landowner/Occupier-Special Duty)	MP summer lodge B city folk/guest (Invitee?) Manager suggested tent 1977 bear attack	Liable
	Breach	Manager knew of 1977 bear attack B city folk	
	Causation Actual	 No warning (but for)	
	Proximate	Remote section of wilderness 1977 bear attack (foreseeable?) Injuries (result)	
	Damages	Bear attack/severe injuries (general) $10,000 medicals (special) $2,000 lost income (special) $1,000 travel expenses (special)	
STRICT LIABILITY	Landowner	Mountain Pines	No Liability
	Known Dangerous Propensities	Known 1977 bear attack Tent adjacent to lodge	
	Wild Animals Maintained On Premises	Bear attack Ø	

EXAMPLE OF IRAC CONTRACTS ISSUE

(I) **Breach**

(R) A breach is (1) an unjustified failure to perform which goes to (2) the essence of the bargain.

(A) When the Browns arrived at the lodge in the early afternoon of June 1, 1978 and were informed that their reservations could not be honored, Mountain Pines' refusal was (1) an unjustified failure to perform as promised.

Since they were given a tent instead of a room, the failure went to (2) the essence of the bargain.

Mountain Pines may counter that the Browns were given a tent for only one night out of seven and, thus, the failure of performance was a minor deviation.

However, since the Browns were "city folks" who were inexperienced in the wilderness, even one night in a tent in a forested area was major.

(C) Therefore, Mountain Pines breached its duty to perform

SUGGESTED MODEL ANSWER

BROWNS v. MOUNTAIN PINES

Claims for Relief

CONTRACT LIABILITY

Offer

An offer is an outward manifestation of intent to be bound by contractual agreement requiring definite and certain terms communicated to the offeree.

Mr. Brown learned of a summer lodge called Mountain Pines. When he wrote to Mountain Pines describing himself as a "city folk" and requested a reservation, his conduct and language in the letter demonstrated his outward manifestation of intent to be bound to a rental agreement.

Mr. Brown specified a quantity, one room rental, time, June 1-8, 1978, identity of parties, Mr./Mrs. Brown and Mountain Pines. Though the price was not stated, Mr. Brown enclosed a $100.00 deposit for a rental price that would be reasonably implied for a popular summer lodge and stated the subject matter as one reservation. Since these terms were mentioned with particularity, they were definite and certain.

Mr. Brown's letter was sent to and received by Mountain Pines, which demonstrates a communication to the offeree.

Therefore, a valid offer exists.

Acceptance

Acceptance is an unequivocal assent to the terms of the offer.

When Mountain Pines acknowledged receipt of the deposit and confirmed the requested reservation by return postcard, their conduct and language constituted an unequivocal assent to the terms of the offer.

Mountain Pines will counter that an additional term of $500.00 was added and changed the term of price. Thus, there was no unequivocal assent to original terms of the offer. However, since Mountain Pines was merely clarifying the price based on the $100.00 deposit, it would not be treated as an additional term.

Therefore, the postcard was a valid acceptance.

Consideration

Consideration is that which is bargained for and given in exchange for a return promise requiring benefit or detriment.

Mr. Brown's promise to pay $500.00 was bargained for in exchange for Mountain Pine's return promise to reserve a room. His detriment would be a financial obligation and his benefit would be a confirmed reservation. Mountain Pine's detriment would be the inability to rent the room to another renter from June 1-8, 1978. Its benefit would be the deposit and final payment.

Therefore, valid consideration exists.

Modification

A modification is a change in the terms of the original offer requiring mutual assent and consideration.

When the Browns arrived at Mountain Pines on June 1, 1978, they were informed by the apologetic manager that their reservation could not be honored because all rooms were occupied. The manager suggested that, as an alternative, the Browns stay overnight in a tent in a forested area adjacent to the lodge. His suggestion demonstrated an offer to change the terms of the original offer. The Browns agreed to the new terms by paying the cost of the tent accommodations which would equate to mutual assent.

The Browns will counter that when they agreed, they did so reluctantly. They were city folks in a remote section of the wilderness and their agreement resulted from a lack of choice. Therefore, there was no mutual assent.

Furthermore, since Mountain Pines was under a pre-existing duty to provide them with a confirmed room, it suffered no detriment by attempting to put them in a tent outside of the lodge. Thus, there was no new consideration for the changed terms.

The modification was invalid.

Waiver

A waiver is a voluntary relinquishment of a known right.

Mountain Pines will contend that when the Browns agreed to stay in the tent, they voluntarily relinquished their known right to a room.

However, as previously stated, since they had no other choice, their relinquishment of the room was not voluntary.

Therefore, there was no waiver.

Statute of Frauds

Contracts that cannot be fully performed within one year require a writing to memorialize the agreement.

Mr. Brown wrote to Mountain Pines in January of 1977 requesting a room reservation in June, 1978. Based on these dates, Mountain Pines will argue that the contract cannot be performed within one year and is, thus, barred by the Statute of Frauds.

Sufficient Memorandum

A memorandum of the essential terms of the agreement will satisfy the Statute of Frauds if it is signed by the party to be charged.

Mr. Brown will argue that the postcard sent by Mountain Pines, which confirmed the room reservation and stated the price, contained all of the essential terms of the agreement. Even though it was not signed, the card bore the name of Mountain Pines in print which would constitute an adoptive signature by the party to be charged.

The postcard would be deemed a sufficient memorandum for the purposes of a writing which would satisfy the Statute of Frauds.

Therefore, the Statute of Frauds is an invalid defense.

Breach

A breach is an unjustified failure to perform which goes to the essence of the bargain.

When the Browns arrived at the lodge in the early afternoon of June 1, 1978 and were informed that their reservations could not be honored, Mountain Pines' refusal was an unjustified failure to perform as promised.

Since they were given a tent instead of a room, the failure went to the essence of the bargain.

Mountain Pines may counter that the Browns were given a tent for only one night out of seven and, thus, the failure of performance was a minor deviation.

However, since the Browns were "city folks" who were inexperienced in the wilderness, even one night in a tent in a forested area was major.

Therefore, Mountain Pines breached its duty to perform.

Damages

Breach of contract entitles the non-breaching party to his/her expectancy under the contract.

The Browns are entitled to the recovery of their $100.00 deposit as general damages. The cost of their additional travel expense, which were foreseeable at the original time of contracting, are also recoverable as special damages (**Hadley v. Baxendale**).

Tort Liability

Respondeat Superior

An employer is liable for the acts of its employees while in the course and scope of employment.

The facts indicate that Manager operated the lodge for Mountain Pines, thus, establishing an employer/employee relationship.

The Mountain Pines manager failed to inform the Browns of the known bear attack on guests in a tent in the summer of 1977. When he put them in tent in the same area knowing that they were inexperienced city folks, he was acting within the course and scope of his employment. Thus, Mountain Pines as his employer, will be liable for manager's conduct.

Respondeat Superior will apply.

Negligence

Negligence requires that a duty was owed, that the duty was breached and the breach was the actual and proximate cause of damages.

Special Duty - Landowner/Occupier

Here, Mountain Pines occupied and owned the summer lodge where the Browns were to stay, thus, qualifying as a landowner/occupier. Further, since the Browns were guests and conferred a pecuniary benefit on Mountain Pines, they would be considered invitees.

As invitees, Mountain Pines owed a special duty to inspect its premises and warn its guests of known dangers i.e., bear attacks.

Therefore, Mountain Pines owed a special duty to the Browns.

Breach

When manager failed to inspect and warn the Browns of the danger from bears on the lodge premises even though he knew of the previous bear attack, he did not act as an average reasonable manager under same or similar circumstances.

Mr. Brown had specified in his initial letter that he was a city folk. This would put Mountain Pines on notice that the Browns were inexperienced campers.

Manager's failure to make the premises safe and warn of the known danger would be considered a breach of his duty.

Actual Causation

"But for" manager's failure to warn and make safe, the Browns would not have been attacked in the tent.

Therefore, manager's actions were the actual cause of the Browns' injuries.

Proximate Causation

The Browns will assert that it is foreseeable that when city folks are put in a tent in a remote section of the wilderness where a previous bear attack had occurred, that another attack on guests could happen which would result in physical injuries.

Therefore, manager's act of putting the Browns in the tent was the proximate cause of their injuries.

Damages

The Browns will seek to recover for their pain and suffering as general damages since these damages directly resulted from the bear attack. Further, damages in the amount of $10,000 in medical expenses, $2,000 in lost income and $1,000 in travel expenses appear to be certain, foreseeable, and not too remote. Thus they will be recoverable as special damages.

Mountain Pines is liable for the negligence of its manager.

Strict Liability

A landowner holds absolute liability for injuries resulting from the known dangerous propensities of wild animals that are maintained on his premises.

Since manager knew of the bear attack in 1977, it can be inferred that the landowner, Mountain Pines, was aware that bears frequented its premises. Attacks by bears are the known and dangerous propensity of these animals. Thus, when Mountain Pines put guests in tents on its premises where bears roamed, it would hold absolute liability for resulting injuries.

However, there are no facts to indict Mountain Pines maintained wild bears on it's premises.

Therefore, Mountain Pines may not be liable under the theory of strict liability.

CONTRACTS QUESTION #4

FREECO

Freeco, a charitable organization, received many pledges during its yearly fund raising drive. The following written pledge was received from Tom, "In consideration of the pledges of others, I hereby pledge $20,000 to Freeco. Signed Tom." Freeco immediately forwarded to Tom the required pledge forms for his completion and return.

Tom had developed a manufacturing machine (UMAC) which would be very valuable if its technical problems could be solved. Alex, fully aware of the technical problems, offered to purchase "UMAC" from Tom. Tom stated, "I'll let you have "UMAC" if you agree to pay Freeco the $20,000 that I pledged to it last week." Alex said, "Okay."

Approximately four months later Tom wrote Alex not to pay the $20,000 to Freeco, but to pay it directly to Tom. Alex agreed that he would do so. Two months later, Alex discovered that the technical problems with "UMAC" could not be solved. Alex immediately sent a letter to Tom stating that he was not going to be able to use "UMAC" and that he was not going to pay the $20,000 to either Freeco or Tom.

1. What are Tom's rights against Alex?

2. What are Freeco's rights against Tom?

3. What are Freeco's rights against Alex?

IRAC OUTLINE SHEET

(I)	(R)	(A)	(C)

EXAMPLE OF PROPER IRAC OUTLINE

TOM v. ALEX

(I)	(R)	(A)	(C)
OFFER	Intent	Offered to purchase UMAC Alex offered to purchase UMAC-- knowledge of technical problems	Offer
	Definite/Certain Terms	One machine (quantity) Reasonable time (time) Alex/Tom (parties) No price UMAC (subject matter)	
	Communicated to Offeree	Offered to purchase	
COUNTER OFFER	Words/Conduct	I'll let you have UMAC if you agree to pay Freeco the $20,000 I pledged	Counter Offer
	Understood As Rejection	Alex said OK	
ACCEPTANCE	Unequivocal As Assent	"Okay"	Acceptance
	Terms of Offer	Supra	
CONSIDERATION	Bargained for Exchange (Benefit/Detriment)	Promise to sell UMAC, promise to pay Freeco $20,000 Tom gives up right to UMAC-- Alex incurs a $20,000 debt Tom has debt paid by Alex Alex receives UMAC	Consideration
MODIFICATION	Change In Terms	Alex to pay Tom—not Freeco	Valid Modification
	Mutual Assent	Alex and Tom agree	
	Consideration	Tom receives $20,000—Alex supra	
	U.C.C—Good Faith	Tom forebear right to sue Alex-- (Good Faith?)	
DEFENSE--STATUTE OF FRAUDS	Contract for Good Over $500	UMAC $20,000	Valid Defense
	Writing	Oral agreement	
EXCEPTION-SUFFICIENT MEMORANDUM	Memo With Essential Terms	Alex's letter to Tom "cannot use" UMAC or pay $20,000 to Freeco or Tom	Valid Exception
	Signed by Party Charged	Alex's letter (signed?)	

FREECO v. TOM

(I)	(R)	(A)	(C)
OFFER	Intent	I hereby pledge	Offer
	Definite/Certain Terms	One pledge (quantity) Reasonable time (time) Freeco and Tom (parties) $20,000 (price) Money (subject matter)	
	Communication of Offeree	Written pledge to Freeco	
ACCEPTANCE	Unequivocal Assent	Sent pledge forms	Acceptance
	Terms of Offer	Pledge	

(I)	(R)	(A)	(C)
CONSIDERATION	Bargained for Exchange (Benefit/Detriment)	Promise to pay—in consideration of pledges of others Tom gets tax deduction, Freeco gets $20,000 donation Tom incurs debt, Freeco expends time?	Arguable
PROMISSORY ESTOPPEL	Promise Reasonably Expected To Induce Reliance	Yearly fund raising drive $20,000 pledge Freeco sent pledge forms	Estoppel Valid
	Enforced to Prevent Injustice	$20,000	
FREECO v. ALEX			
THIRD PARTY BENEFICIARY	Rights Arise at Formation Stage	Freeco named in Tom/Alex contract supra	Third Party Beneficiary
PRIVITY	Relationship	(Third party exception)	No Privity Required
INTENT	Promisee's Intent to Benefit	Tom had Alex promise to pay Freeco $20,000	Intent
CLASSIFICATION	Creditor (Discharge A Duty)	Pledge created a $20,000 enforceable debt	Classification--Creditor
	Donee (Confer A Gift)	Pledge	
VESTING	Notice/Assent or	?	Vested
	Bring Suit or	Filed suit after modification	
	Materially Changes Position	Filed suit after modification	
STATUTE OF FRAUDS	Third Party Subject To Promisee's Defenses	Supra	No Defense

EXAMPLE OF IRAC CONTRACTS ISSUE

(I) **Modification**

(R) A modification is (1) a change in the terms of the original offer requiring (2) mutual assent and (3) consideration.

(A) Tom will argue that he wrote with the request that Alex pay the $20,000 directly to him rather than to Freeco as previously agreed. This (1) changed the term of the original offer regarding the party to whom payment was to be made.

Alex agreed to this change in his payment obligation term which demonstrated (2) mutual assent.

Further, Tom would benefit from the direct $20,000 payment, and would suffer detriment by giving up his right to sue Alex for specific performance if he did not pay Freeco. Alex's benefit and detriment would remain the same (supra).

(C) Therefore, sufficient (3) consideration was present to support the modification of the terms of payment in the original contract.

SUGGESTED MODEL ANSWER

1. TOM v. ALEX

Offer

An outward manifestation of intent to be bound by contractual agreement requiring definite and certain terms communicated to the offeree.

Tom will assert that when Alex "offered to purchase" UMAC from him, Alex's communication was an outward manifestation of his intent to enter into a binding contractual agreement with Tom. Alex was aware of the technical problems with UMAC at the time, but this knowledge did not deter his intent to purchase the machine.

Alex will counter he was merely inviting Tom to deal for the purchase of UMAC if it was available for sale. Since no price or time had been mentioned, Alex's communication was only preliminary negotiations.

However, UMAC was a machine. As a good in excess of $500, its sale would be governed by the rules of U.C.C. which do not require that the price and time be given in the initial offer. These terms can be reasonably implied based on the subject matter of the offer and business custom. One UMAC was given as the quantity. The parties were stated as Alex and Tom. Since these terms were specified with particularity, they were definite and certain.

Alex's offer to purchase UMAC was communicated to Tom.

Thus, it was a valid offer.

Counter Offer

Words which a reasonable person would understand as a rejection of the offer is a counter offer.

When Tom stated to Alex, "I'll let you have UMAC if you agree to pay Freeco the $20,000 I pledged...," he added an additional term concerning payment to Freeco. Since the payment to Freeco was not a mirror image of Alex's offer, these words would lead a reasonable person to understand it as a rejection of the offer to purchase unless the payment was to be made to Freeco. Since Alex said "okay" he did, in fact, understand it to be a rejection.

Tom's statement was a sufficient communication to constitute a valid counter offer.

Acceptance

Acceptance is an unequivocal assent to the terms of the offer.

When Alex stated "okay" in response to Tom's counter offer, he unequivocally assented to the terms of the sale.

Therefore, Alex validly accepted the counter offer.

Consideration

Consideration is that which is bargained for and given in exchange for a return promise requiring benefit or detriment.

Tom will assert that Alex bargained for Tom's promise to sell UMAC which was given in exchange for Alex's return promise to pay Freeco $20,000 which Tom had previously pledged.

Alex would benefit by receiving UMAC and would incur the detriment of a $20,000 debt to Freeco which he was not previously obligated to pay.

Tom would benefit from Alex's satisfaction of his $20,000 pledge to Freeco and would incur the detriment of giving up his rights to UMAC.

Thus, valuable consideration was given by both parties sufficient for a valid contract.

Modification

A modification is a change in the terms of the original offer requiring mutual assent and consideration.

Tom will argue that he wrote with the request that Alex pay the $20,000 directly to him rather than to Freeco as previously agreed. This changed the term of the original offer regarding the party to whom payment was to be made.

Alex agreed to this change in his payment obligation term which demonstrated mutual assent.

Further, Tom would benefit from the direct $20,000 payment, and would suffer detriment by giving up his right to sue Alex for specific performance if he did not pay Freeco. Alex's benefit and detriment would remain the same (supra).

Therefore, sufficient consideration was present to support the modification of the terms of payment in the original contract.

Under the rules of U.C.C., the modification would be valid if it was made in good faith. Absent facts to the contrary, the U.C.C. would support the modification.

Defense - Statute of Frauds

A contract for the sale of goods for $500 or more must be in writing.

Alex will assert that the contract involved the sale of UMAC, a good, for $20,000. The contract was oral and, thus, did not satisfy the requirement for a writing.

Therefore, the contract is barred by the Statute of Frauds.

Exception - Sufficient Memorandum

A memorandum of the essential terms of the agreement will satisfy the Statute of Frauds if it is signed by the party to be charged.

Alex's rejection letter sent to Tom stating "not able to use UMAC and not going to pay $20,000 to Freeco or Tom" sufficiently identified all the essential terms of the offer. Assuming that Alex signed it, the letter would constitute a sufficient memorandum and would bring the contract outside of the Statute of Frauds.

Exception - Receipt of Goods

When the buyer receives and accepts all or part of the goods, the contract will not be barred by the Statute of Frauds.

Approximately six months had elapsed from the formation of the contract. Since Alex discovered that UMAC's technical problems could not be solved during that time, it can be inferred that he had received and accepted the machine. If so, his receipt of UMAC would take the sale out of the Statute of Frauds.

The Statute of Frauds will not apply.

2. FREECO v. TOM

Offer

Defined supra.

Freeco will contend that Tom's language in his written pledge, "I hereby pledge $20,000 in consideration of the pledges of others," was an outward manifestation demonstrating his present intent to be bound by contractual agreement.

The terms of the promise were stated as to the quantity (one), time of performance (implied as to reasonable time), identity of parties (Freeco and Tom), price ($20,000), and subject matter (pledge). Since these terms were stated with particularity, they were definite and certain. The pledge was sent by Tom and received by Freeco demonstrating communication.

Tom's pledge was a valid offer.

Acceptance

Defined supra.

The facts indicate that Freeco immediately forwarded the required pledge forms to Tom which was the usual method of assent to a pledge.

This immediate response was an unequivocal and unqualified acceptance of Tom's $20,000 pledge.

Thus, Freeco's acceptance was effective.

Consideration

Defined supra.

Freeco will argue that Tom's promise to pay $20,000 was bargained for on the basis of his own language "in consideration of the pledges of others."

Freeco would benefit from the $20,000 donation for its charitable activities. It would incur detriment from the time expenditure necessary to send out the pledge forms for collection of the obligation.

Tom's <u>benefit</u> from the pledge would include the feeling of well being associated with charitable donations and any allowable <u>tax</u> <u>deductions</u>. He would incur the <u>detriment</u> of a $20,000 <u>debt</u>. Therefore, sufficient consideration seems to be present to enforce the contract.

However, if the court should find that Freeco did <u>not</u> suffer <u>sufficient</u> <u>detriment</u>, Freeco would proceed on the theory of <u>promissory</u> <u>estoppel</u>.

<u>Promissory Estoppel</u>

A <u>promise</u> which the promisor should <u>reasonably</u> <u>expect</u> to <u>induce</u> <u>action</u> or <u>forbearance</u> on the part of the <u>promisee/third</u> <u>party</u> which <u>does</u> <u>induce</u> such <u>action/forbearance</u> is <u>binding</u> if <u>injustice</u> can be <u>avoided</u> only by <u>enforcement</u> of the <u>promise</u>.

Freeco will contend that <u>Tom</u> <u>knew</u> that Freeco was involved in its yearly fund drive and would <u>use</u> his $20,000 <u>pledge</u> as an <u>example</u> to other prospective donees to <u>induce</u> them to <u>pledge</u> as much or more. Freeco's <u>reliance</u> <u>induced</u> them to <u>send</u> him pledge <u>forms</u> which would undoubtedly be used as part of the campaign drive.

Further, its <u>reliance</u> was both <u>reasonable</u> and <u>foreseeable</u> because it was actively encouraged by Tom's written pledge (supra).

Therefore, despite any absence of consideration, Tom should be <u>estopped</u> from <u>revoking</u> his <u>donation</u> to <u>avoid</u> the <u>injustice</u> that would be created by Freeco's <u>detrimental</u> <u>reliance</u>.

Thus, Tom will be estopped from revoking his donation.

3. <u>FREECO v. ALEX</u>

<u>Third Party Beneficiary</u>

A third party beneficiary contract is one wherein <u>performance</u> by the <u>promisor</u> will <u>benefit</u> a <u>third</u> <u>party</u>. His <u>status</u> <u>arises</u> at the <u>formation</u> <u>stage</u> of the contract.

As part of his contract with Tom, Alex <u>agreed</u> to <u>pay</u> the <u>$20,000</u> purchase price for UMAC to <u>Freeco</u>. The <u>performance</u> of this <u>promise</u> was meant to fulfill Tom's pledge obligation which would act to the <u>benefit</u> of Freeco, the <u>third</u> <u>party</u>.

<u>Freeco's</u> <u>rights</u> were created at the time that Tom contracted with Alex. Its status <u>arose</u> at the <u>formation</u> <u>stage</u> of the contract.

Therefore, Freeco may have enforceable rights as a third party beneficiary.

<u>Privity of Contract</u>

Privity of contract is the <u>interest</u> or <u>relationship</u> which exists <u>between</u> two or more <u>contracting</u> <u>parties</u>.

Alex will assert that Freeco was <u>not</u> a <u>party</u> to the <u>original</u> <u>contract</u> and, therefore, has <u>no</u> <u>interest</u> or <u>relationship</u> in that contract upon which to sue.

Freeco will rebut that although it was <u>not</u> a <u>party</u> to the original <u>Tom/Alex</u> <u>contract</u>, <u>privity</u> is <u>not</u> <u>required</u> for it to assert its rights as a <u>third</u> <u>party</u> <u>beneficiary</u> as set forth in the case of **<u>Lawrence v. Fox.</u>**

Thus, the lack of privity will not bar Freeco from asserting its rights.

Intent to Benefit

Intent to benefit is defined as the promisee's intent to extract a promise from the promisor to benefit a third party.

Freeco will contend that when Tom extracted Alex's promise to pay the $20,000 to Freeco, he intended to benefit it. This promise was made at the time of the Tom/Alex contract which further demonstrates Tom's beneficial intent.

Classification - Creditor Beneficiary

If the promisee's primary intent is to discharge a duty owed to the third party, the third party is a creditor beneficiary.

Alex will argue that Tom's pledge created a debt owed to Freeco. Tom believed the obligation had to be satisfied as demonstrated by his agreement with Alex. When he contracted to have Alex pay Freeco the $20,000, he intended to discharge his obligation actually owed to Freeco as discussed supra.

Therefore, Freeco should be classified as a creditor beneficiary.

Freeco will counter that Tom's intent when he contracted with Alex was to confer upon Freeco the right against Alex to collect the $20,000 donation which Tom had pledged. Since a pledge usually carries with it the recognition of the right to performance in the beneficiary, Freeco may be classified as a donee beneficiary.

However, due to Freeco's enforceable contract right, as discussed supra, its status would be that of a creditor beneficiary.

Vesting

The Restatement Second states that the rights of any intended beneficiary vest when he has notice of and assents to the promise or brings suit to enforce the promise or materially changes position in justifiable reliance thereon.

If the court should rule that Freeco was a creditor beneficiary, Freeco will argue that although it had no notice and did not assent to the Tom/Alex contract, when it filed suit against Alex, such action caused a material change in its legal position at which point its rights vested.

Alex will counter that for Freeco's rights to vest, its change in position would have had to occur prior to the modification. Alex will contend that Freeco filed suit after the modification. Therefore, its rights had not vested, giving Freeco no rights against Alex.

Thus, even though Freeco's rights did not vest as a third party beneficiary, as a creditor, it can still sue Tom under the original obligation.

Defense - Statute of Frauds

The third party beneficiary takes subject to the promisor's defenses assertable against the promisee.

Alex would argue the previously discussed defenses asserted under the Statute of Frauds since these defenses could be used against Tom. However, for reasons discussed supra, the Statute of Frauds would not apply.

CONTRACTS QUESTION #5

FARGO v. TOM

Tom was in his last semester of law school. RIP was a commercial bar review course. On 4/1/79 Tom and RIP entered into a valid written contract whereby Tom agreed to pay RIP $500 and RIP agreed to loan Tom a complete set of its course materials and to provide a 7-week course of instruction starting 6/5/79. This contract contained a clause that read, "This contract may not be assigned".

On 4/15/79 RIP obtained $20,000 financing for its operations from Fargo Bank. In conjunction with this transaction RIP executed the following written instrument: "RIP hereby transfers to Fargo Bank all its right, title, and interest under its 4/1/79 contract with Tom". On 5/1/79 Tom received a copy of this document.

On 5/15/79 Tom received the RIP course materials. On 6/5/79 Tom started attending the RIP lectures. He continued to attend faithfully until 7/20/79, the next-to-last day of the scheduled lectures. During the early morning hours of that day, the RIP lecture hall burned to the ground due to an act of God.

After unsuccessful efforts to obtain another suitable lecture hall, RIP contacted its competitor FAIL. For a consideration FAIL agreed to admit RIP's students to FAIL's lectures in the area of law scheduled for the last two days of the RIP course. Tom did not attend these substitute lectures, which followed a different format than that of RIP materials. Tom has refused to pay Fargo Bank anything.

What are Fargo Bank's rights against Tom? Discuss.

IRAC OUTLINE SHEET

(I)	(R)	(A)	(C)

EXAMPLE OF PROPER IRAC OUTLINE

FARGO BANK v. TOM

(I)	(R)	(A)	(C)
VALIDITY OF CONTRACT	Mutual Assent	RIP provide 7 week course 4/1/79 valid written contract	Valid Contract
	Consideration	Services in exchange for payment	
STANDING	Privity	Fargo Bank not party to 4/1/79 contract	Standing
	Assignment Exception	Assignee (Infra)	
ASSIGNABLE RIGHTS	Contract Right Too Personal	Right to receive $500 from Tom Payment promised to RIP alter performance?	Assignable
	Prohibited by Contract (Right/Power)	"Contract may not be assigned" 5/1/79 notice to Tom	
PRESENT ASSIGNMENT	Intent to Transfer	4/15/79 written instrument RIP hereby transfers rights, etc. 5/1/79 notification	Valid Assignment
	Existing Rights	Right to receive $500	
CONDITIONS (EXPRESS/CONSTRUCTIVE)	Happening/Non-happening Event	Provided Tom with course materials 61/2 weeks from RIP 2 days from FAIL (Condition precedent?)	Condition
	Creates Duty To Perform	7 week course Course materials Pay $500	
COMPLETE PERFORMANCE	Condition Fully Satisfied	See facts under Conditions	No Complete Performance
DELEGATION DUTY	Too Personal	7 week lecture course by RIP FAIL's lecture followed different format	Invalid Delegation-- No Complete Performance
	Prohibited by Contract	Anti-assignment clause (supra) Tom refused to attend substitute lectures	
SUBSTANTIAL PERFORMANCE	Constructive Condition	Supra	Substantial Performance
	Defendant Received Substantial Bargain	Received course materials Received 6 $^{1/2}$ weeks lecture	
	Reimbursed	Reduction in value of two days	
	Hardship to Plaintiff	Forfeit $500	
	Not Willful	Lecture hall burned Act of God Unsuccessful effort to find substitute hall Contacted competitor FAIL Valuable consideration FAIL admit RIP students in area of law schedule	

(I)	(R)	(A)	(C)
DISCHARGED--IMPOSSIBILITY PERFORMANCE	Event	Destruction of lecture hall	Duty Discharged as to Last Two Days
	Performance Impossible	Last two days/partial	
		Tom's payment not impossible	
BREACH	Unjustified Failure to Perform	Tom refused to pay $500	Breach
	Essence of Bargain	RIP performed for money	
DAMAGES	Expectancy Under Contract	$500 less value of last two days	Liable

EXAMPLE OF IRAC CONTRACTS ISSUE

(I) **Did RIP Satisfy The Condition Through Substantial Performance?**

(R) A constructive condition will be satisfied by substantial performance (1) the defendant got substantially what he bargained for, (2) if he can be reimbursed for what he did not receive, (3) if there will be a great hardship to the plaintiff if he is denied recovery under the contract, and (4) the deviation was not willful.

(A) As previously stated, RIP's duty to perform was a constructive condition precedent.

Fargo Bank will assert that Tom received a complete set of RIP's course materials and more than $6^{1/2}$ weeks of a seven week course which was (1) substantially what he had bargained for.

Further, Tom could be given (2) a reduction in the price of the course for the reasonable value of the two days that he did not receive.

In addition, if Fargo Bank was denied recovery of the $500, it would forfeit a substantial sum of money which would be a (3) great financial hardship.

Finally, RIP had not performed the final two days of lecture because its lecture hall had burned down due to an act of God. RIP was in no way at fault. RIP made every effort to locate a substitute hall but when its efforts failed, RIP paid FAIL valuable consideration so that RIP's students would be admitted to the area of law scheduled on the last two days of lecture. Thus, the deviation was (4) not willful but was instead made in good faith.

(C) Therefore, the constructive condition precedent was satisfied through substantial performance.

SUGGESTED MODEL ANSWER

FARGO BANK v. TOM

Validity of Contract

A valid contract requires a showing of mutual assent and consideration.

Fargo Bank will argue that the 4/1/79 agreement was a valid written contract containing all the essential terms sufficient for mutual assent. RIP's agreement to provide Tom with a seven week bar review course with corresponding materials in exchange for Tom's agreement to pay $500 for the course indicates consideration.

Therefore, a valid contract existed.

Does Fargo Bank have Standing to Sue?

There must be privity of contract between the plaintiff and defendant in any contract action.

Fargo Bank will argue that although it was not a party to the original 4/1/79 contract, as RIP's assignee (infra), Fargo Bank is not require to be in privity of contract with Tom.

Therefore, Fargo Bank has standing to sue.

Are the Rights Assignable?

Contract rights are assignable if they are not too personal or prohibited by contract.

Fargo Bank will contend that the contract right to be assigned was the right to receive $500 from Tom which was not too personal to assign.

Tom will counter that he had promised to pay the money to RIP, not Fargo Bank. If he was required to pay a different party, his performance would be altered.

However, payment to Fargo Bank instead of RIP would not materially alter the performance. The price for the course and the time of payment would remain unchanged.

Therefore, the right to collect $500 was not too personal.
Finally, Tom will assert that RIP promised not to assign its rights in the 4/1/79 contract as evidenced by the term "This contract may not be assigned." Thus, RIP had no right to assign the contract to Fargo Bank, as it was prohibited by contract.

However, even though the clause may have destroyed the right to assign, it did not contain language stating "all assignments are null and void" -- the power to assign was still effective and not prohibited by contract.

When Tom received notice of the assignment on 5/1/79 but failed to protest, he implicitly assented to the transfer and, thus, waived his right to enforce the clause.

Therefore, RIP retained the power to assign its rights to Fargo Bank although it would remain liable for damages resulting from breach of the promise not to assign.

Has There Been a Valid Present Assignment?

An assignment requires a present intention to transfer existing rights from the assignor to the assignee.

When RIP executed the 4/15/79 written instrument containing the words, "RIP hereby transfers to Fargo Bank all rights, title, and interest under the 4/11/79 contract", this language manifested RIP's (assignor) present intent to transfer the existing right to receive the $500 from Tom to Fargo Bank (assignee). RIP's act of notifying Tom of the transfer on 5/1/79 further indicated RIP's present intent to create an effective assignment.

The instrument extinguished RIP's right to the money and transferred the existing right to Fargo Bank. Fargo Bank, in effect, "stepped into RIP's shoes" and assumed all the rights of enforcement that RIP had prior to the transfer.

Therefore, there was a valid present assignment.

Were There Any Conditions to Tom's Performance?

A condition is a fact or event, the happening or non-happening of which either creates or extinguishes an absolute duty to perform.

Tom will contend that his duty to pay was conditioned upon his receipt of the seven week course with corresponding materials from RIP. This express condition would have to be fully performed by RIP before his duty to pay would arise.

However, the contract did not contain express language that Tom would pay "only if" RIP fully performed. The contract simply stated that Tom and RIP "agreed" to reciprocal performances.

Thus, RIP's duty to perform appears to be an implied constructive condition precedent to Tom's duty to pay...

Was The Condition Satisfied Through Complete Performance?

Complete performance occurs when the condition has fully performed.

Fargo Bank will argue that RIP had provided Tom with the complete set of course materials on 5/15/79. It had given him the seven week course which had consisted of $6^{1/2}$ weeks of lecture by RIP and two days of lecture by FAIL, a competitor who provided a similar bar review as that given by RIP.

Therefore, Tom had received complete performance.

Tom will counter that the last two days of lecture were not performed by RIP.

Thus, there was no complete performance.

Delegation of Duty

A duty may be delegated unless the duty is too personal or prohibited by contract.

Tom will assert that he had bargained for RIP's seven week course which was unique in its methods of bar review instruction. Its lectures corresponded to its course materials and any attempt to delegate the lecture duties to FAIL would interrupt the consistency of instruction.

Further, FAIL's lectures followed a different format from RIP's material which materially varied the instruction promised by RIP.

Therefore, the lecture duties were too personal to delegate to FAIL. As a result, Tom did not receive RIP's complete performance.

Effect of Anti-Assignment Clause

Anti-assignment clause is to be interpreted as forbidding delegation of duties

Tom will argue that the anti-assignment clause (supra) forbade any delegation of RIP duty to perform the contract which included the last two days of lecture.

Fargo Bank will counter that the clause did not specifically state that delegation duties was prohibited.

However, as a matter of public policy, anti-assignment clauses are to be interpreted as forbidding delegation of contract duties unless otherwise stipulated.

Therefore, since Tom asserted his right to refuse the delegation by failing to attend the substitute lectures, he enforced the prohibition against delegation of duties under the anti-assignment clause. His refusal resulted in RIP's failure of performance for the final two days of the course.

RIP's attempt to delegate was improper.

Did RIP Satisfy the Condition Through Substantial Performance?

A constructive condition will be satisfied by substantial performance if the defendant got substantially what he bargained for, if he can be reimbursed for what he did not receive, if there will be a great hardship to the plaintiff if he is denied recovery under the contract, and the deviation was not willful.

As previously stated, RIP's duty to perform was a constructive condition precedent.

Fargo Bank will assert that Tom received a complete set of RIP's course materials and more than $6^{1/2}$ weeks of a seven week course which was substantially what he had bargained for.

Further, Tom could be given a reduction in the price of the course for the reasonable value of the two days that he did not receive.

In addition, if Fargo Bank was denied recovery of the $500, it would forfeit a substantial sum of money which would be a great financial hardship.

Finally, RIP had not performed the final two days of lecture because its lecture hall had burned down due to an act of God. RIP was in no way at fault. RIP made every effort to locate a substitute hall but when its efforts failed, RIP paid FAIL valuable consideration so that RIP's students would be admitted to the area of law scheduled on the last two days of lecture. Thus, the deviation was not willful but was instead made in good faith.

Therefore, the constructive condition precedent was satisfied through substantial performance.

Was Tom's Duty Discharged Through Impossibility of Performance?

A promisor's duty to perform will be discharged after a contract has been entered into if, due to an event, performance becomes objectively impossible to accomplish.

Tom will argue that RIP could not perform the final two days of lecture due to the destruction of its only available lecture hall. Complete performance was objectively impossible since it couldn't find another hall.

Therefore, Tom's duty to pay was discharged.

Fargo Bank will counter that the impossibility involved only the last two days of lecture and was, therefore, a mere partial impossibility as to these final lectures. Tom's own performance i.e., payment of the reasonable value of what he had received, was not impossible.

Therefore, Tom's duty to pay would be discharged only as to the last two days of lecture.

Breach

A breach is an unjustified failure to perform which goes to the essence of the bargain.

Fargo Bank will argue that Tom's unjustified failure to pay the $500 for the bar review went to the essence of the bargain since RIP would not have otherwise performed.

Therefore, Tom's refusal to pay was a material breach of his duty to perform.

Damages

Breach of contract entitles the non-breaching party to his/her expectancy under the contract.

Fargo Bank will seek damages in the amount of $500 which is its expectancy under the contract, less the amount representing the reasonable value of the last two days of instruction.

Damages will be awarded.

SECTION VII

CRIMINAL LAW

CRIMINAL LAW

LEARN TO WRITE THE RIGHT WAY®

CRIMINAL LAW QUESTION #1

STATE v. DAN

Bob, an undercover police officer, learned from informers that Dan had been claiming to be a mob "hit man" who would kill for a price. Bob spread the word that he wanted Vic killed. Hearing this, Dan approached Bob and offered to kill Vic for $10,000. Bob told Dan he would pay this amount. Bob agreed to act as a lookout on the next afternoon and promised to signal Dan when Vic left his office so that Dan would be able to follow Vic to a remote location where Dan could kill Vic. Bob knew that Vic was away on vacation and would not return for two weeks. He arranged for other officers to arrest Dan at the stakeout.

On the next day, each went to the agreed location. After a short wait, Dan concluded he had been tricked. He accused Bob of being a police agent, and threatened Bob with a pistol. The pistol accidentally discharged, wounding Bob. Dan was arrested by the arriving officers. The ambulance which was transporting Bob to the hospital was hit by a truck. Bob was killed instantly.

Dan has been charged with conspiracy to murder Vic, attempted murder of Vic, and murder of Bob.

1. Should the court grant Dan's request that the jury be instructed on the defense of entrapment? Discuss.

2. If Dan is not successful in offering an entrapment defense, and the facts set out above are established by competent evidence, may Dan properly be convicted of:

    a. Conspiracy to murder Vic? Discuss.
    b. Attempted murder of Vic? Discuss.
    c. Murder of Bob? Discuss.

IRAC OUTLINE SHEET

(I)	(R)	(A)	(C)

EXAMPLE OF PROPER IRAC OUTLINE

STATE v. DAN

(I)	(R)	(A)	(C)
ENTRAPMENT	Traditional View (Subjective)		
	Instigation	B undercover agent learned from informers D claiming "hit man/kill for $" B spread word he wanted V killed	No Defense
	Predisposition	Hearing, D approached B/offered to kill for $10,000 B told D he would pay	
	Modern View (Objective)		
	Law Enforcement Activity	Undercover officer B spread word (Supra) D sought job "hit man"	
CONSPIRACY	Agreement	D approached B/offered to kill V for $10,000 B told D he would pay B agreed to act as lookout/signal	Split of Jurisdictions
	Two or More Persons	B undercover agent (feigned accomplice) D hit man	
	Specific Intent/Unlawful Act	Kill V for money	
ATTEMPTED MURDER	Specific Intent	Supra	No Attempted Murder
	Legal/Factual Impossibility	V away on vacation/not return for two weeks (factual)	
	Apparent Ability	D went to V's office	
	Preparation/Perpetration	D went to agreed location B acted as lookout/to signal D waited- V on vacation Follow V to remote location	
MURDER OF BOB			
HOMICIDE	Killing of Another	D wounded B with pistol B killed instantly/ambulance accident	Homicide
	Causation		
	Actual	"But For" pistol discharge/wounding	
	Proximate	D threatened B with a pistol Accidentally discharged/wounded B Ambulance transporting B hit/B killed (intervening acts?)	
MURDER	Killing of Another	Supra	Arguable
	Malice		
	Specific Intent To Cause Serious Bodily Harm	Threatened B with pistol	
	Willful/Wanton Conduct	Pistol accidentally discharged/wounded	
FIRST DEGREE MURDER	Specific Intent to Kill	Pistol accidentally discharged	No First Degree Murder
	Premeditation/Deliberation	Ø	
SECOND DEGREE MURDER	All Murder Not First Degree	Supra	Second Degree Murder

(I)	(R)	(A)	(C)
VOLUNTARY MANSLAUGHTER	Adequate Provocation	D concluded he had been tricked Accused B of being police agent Threatened with a pistol Accidental discharge	No Voluntary Manslaughter
INVOLUNTARY MANSLAUGHTER	Unintentional Killing Without Malice (Criminal Negligence)	Threatened B with a pistol Pistol accidentally discharged	Arguable

EXAMPLE OF IRAC CRIMINAL LAW ISSUE

(I) **Attempted Murder**

(R) An attempt requires (1) the specific intent to commit a crime, (2) a factual impossibility preventing its completion, coupled with (3) the apparent ability in combination with (4) acts that go beyond mere preparation entering the zone of perpetration.

(A) Dan had (1) the specific intent to kill as discussed supra.

His mere presence at the agreed location for the purpose of accomplishing the task was illegal. Thus, the killing was legally possible.

Dan may rebut that because Vic was away on vacation for two weeks on the night of the proposed killing, it was (2) factually impossible for him to commit the crime. However, factual impossibility is no defense to an attempt.

When Dan went to Vic's office to wait for him so he could follow him to a remote area to complete the "kill," he had (3) the apparent ability to commit the crime.

Finally, Dan waited at the agreed location where he was to find and follow Vic. The kill was to take place in a remote location away from Vic's office. It was necessary for Bob to act as a lookout and signal Vic as the target. Thus, it appears that Dan was (4) merely preparing to follow Vic. He had taken no further steps in perpetration of the actual killing.

(C) Therefore, Dan may not be convicted of attempted murder.

SUGGESTED MODEL ANSWER

STATE v. DAN

1. Entrapment

Entrapment exists at common law, if a law enforcement officer has instigated the commission of an offense in the mind of a person who was not otherwise predisposed to commit crimes; or modernly, if law enforcement's conduct results in the inducement of the commission of a crime.

Under the traditional view, Dan will argue that Bob, an undercover police officer, learned from informers that Dan was a "hit man." In an effort to instigate Dan to commit the act, Bob had spread the word that he wanted Vic killed for a price. Bob's activity as a law enforcement officer created the intent in the mind of Dan to commit the crime.

However, Bob had merely "spread the word." He did not approach Dan or personally contact him in an effort to instigate Dan to commit the killing. It was only after Dan approached Bob and offered to kill Vic for $10,000 that Bob told him he would pay. Thus, the intent to kill for money was already in Dan's mind and he actively sought out the opportunity to commit the act.

Further, Dan had claimed to be a mob "hit man" who would kill for a price as reported by police informers. These facts coupled with Dan's conduct of approaching Bob and offering to do the "kill", illustrates that he was not otherwise an innocent person. Rather, his conduct and reputation indicates his predisposition to commit this sort of crime.

Even under the modern view which takes an objective approach to the conduct of the officer, Bob's conduct was merely "spreading the word." He did not persuade or urge Dan to perpetrate the killing.

A reasonable person, who was otherwise innocent, would not have been likely to respond to this information by actively seeking out the "job" to kill Vic.

Under either view, entrapment will not be a valid defense. The court should not grant Dan's request.

2.(a) Conspiracy

A conspiracy is an agreement between two or more persons with the specific intent to commit an unlawful act.

When Dan approached Bob and offered to kill Vic for $10,000 to which Bob responded that he would pay, an agreement was formed between two or more persons.

However, Bob was an undercover officer posing as a criminal and was, thus, a feigned accomplice. As such, a plurality of two or more persons with the requisite mens rea to kill was not satisfied in the majority of jurisdictions.

In a minority of jurisdictions, an agreement by the defendant alone is sufficient to satisfy an agreement between the two parties, even in the situation where a feigned accomplice is involved. Since Dan intended to kill Vic for $10,000, he had the requisite specific intent to commit the unlawful act of murder.

In a minority of jurisdictions, Dan may be convicted of conspiracy.

(b) Attempted Murder

An attempt requires the specific intent to commit a crime, a factual impossibility preventing its completion, coupled with the apparent ability in combination with acts that go beyond mere preparation entering the zone of perpetration.

Dan had the specific intent to kill as discussed supra.

His mere presence at the agreed location for the purpose of accomplishing the task was illegal. Thus, the killing was legally possible.

Dan may rebut that because Vic was away on vacation for two weeks on the night of the proposed killing it was factually impossible for him to commit the crime. However, factual impossibility is no defense to an attempt.

When Dan went to Vic's office to wait for him so he could follow him to a remote area to complete the "kill," he had the apparent ability to commit the crime.

Finally, Dan waited at the agreed location where he was to find and follow Vic. The kill was to take place in a remote location away from Vic's office. It was necessary for Bob to act as a lookout and signal Vic as the target. Thus, it appears that Dan was merely preparing to follow Vic. He had taken no further steps in perpetration of the actual killing.

Therefore, Dan may not be convicted of attempted murder.

(c) Murder of Bob

Homicide

Homicide is the killing of one human being by another human being.

Bob was wounded by Dan and subsequently killed in an ambulance accident. Thus, a killing occurred.

Actual Causation

"But for" Bob's wounding Dan, his death would not have happened in the ambulance accident. Dan is, thus, the actual cause of Bob's death.

Proximate Causation

When Dan used a loaded pistol to threaten Bob, it was foreseeable that it could accidentally discharge resulting in severe injury or death.

Dan will counter that it was the ambulance accident rather than the wounding that resulted in Bob's instantaneous death. This accident was an intervening act which came into play after the actions of Dan and should sever the chain of causation.

However, severe injury or death was a foreseeable result of Dan's use of the pistol. The sequence of events due to the ambulance accident may not have been anticipated. Nonetheless, they were the natural and probable consequence of the need for hospitalization due to the injuries sustained and would, thus, be foreseeable. Dan would not be relieved of liability. Dan is the proximate cause of Bob's death.

A homicide has been committed.

Murder

Murder is an unlawful killing of another with malice aforethought.

A killing has been established supra. When Dan threatened Bob with a loaded pistol, his use of such a dangerous weapon shows a specific intent to cause serious bodily harm sufficient to prove malice aforethought.

Dan will assert that the pistol accidentally discharged. He only meant to scare Bob by his threats with the pistol but had no specific intent to cause serious bodily harm.

However, the mere use of the weapon to threaten Bob, which always carries with it the potential of accidental discharge, shows Dan's reckless disregard for human life. At a minimum, this equates to wanton conduct through which malice aforethought can be established.

Dan may be convicted of murder.

First Degree Murder

First degree murder is one committed with the specific intent to kill, plus premeditation and deliberation.

Because the pistol accidentally discharged, there is no showing of a specific intent to kill plus premeditation and deliberation.

Therefore, Dan may not be convicted of murder in the first degree.

Second Degree Murder

Second degree murder is all murder that is not murder in the first degree.

If the prosecution can establish murder as discussed supra, Dan may be convicted of second degree murder.

Voluntary Manslaughter

Voluntary manslaughter is a killing that would otherwise be murder but for some legally recognized form of mitigation.

Adequate Provocation

Dan will assert that when he concluded that he had been tricked by Bob, he became mad. He lost control and acted rashly by accusing Bob of being a police agent and threatening him with the pistol.

Bob's trickery, in fact, provoked his response. He immediately acted before he had sufficient time to cool off, at which point the gun accidentally discharged.

However, trickery is not adequate provocation sufficient to inflame the passions of a reasonable man into killing.

Therefore, Dan's crime should not be mitigated to voluntary manslaughter.

Involuntary Manslaughter

Involuntary manslaughter is an unintentional killing without malice.

If the prosecution cannot prove a murder through malice aforethought (supra), Dan will argue that he only meant to threaten Bob with the pistol.

The accidental discharge of the pistol with the resultant death was an unintended killing brought about in a criminally negligent manner.

Therefore, absent malice, Dan may be guilty of involuntary manslaughter.

CRIMINAL LAW QUESTION #2

STATE v. DAVE

Dave had arranged with the Fine Arts Gallery to inspect, after its nighttime closing, the hanging of Old Masters paintings he had loaned the gallery. While en route to the gallery for such purpose he saw Amos, a rival art collector. Dave suspected that Amos had in some way obtained from Dave's office his only memorandum of the address of an obscure art dealer who possessed, without realizing its value, a painting both Dave and Amos coveted. Dave stepped up behind Amos and stuck his pipe in Amos' back, saying, "Don't move or I'll shoot". As Amos raised his arms, Dave slipped the billfold from Amos' pocket and ran off. He took only the memorandum from the billfold, then threw the billfold with the other contents intact under a street light where he expected Amos to find it.

Dave proceeded to the Fine Arts Gallery where he found the door broken open and the guard, who resided there, bleeding and unconscious from a head wound. Dave grabbed a lance from an exhibit and dashed into the room where his paintings were hanging. There he saw Bob slashing the paintings. Dave was too stunned to react for a moment but he recovered quickly and threw the lance as Bob slashed another painting. The lance killed Bob.

With what crimes can Dave reasonably be charged, and what defenses might reasonably be raised? Discuss.

IRAC OUTLINE SHEET

(I)	(R)	(A)	(C)

EXAMPLE OF PROPER IRAC OUTLINE

STATE v. DAVE

(I)	(R)	(A)	(C)
ROBBERY OF BILLFOLD	Trespassory Taking	Slipped billfold from pocket	Robbery
	Carrying Away	Ran off	
	Personal Property of Another	Amos' billfold	
	Force or Fear	Stuck pipe in back Amos raised arms Don't move or I'll shoot	
	Specific Intent to Deprive (Risk of Loss)	Threw under street light Expected Amos to find it	
ROBBERY OF MEMO	Trespassory Taking	D suspected Amos took memo from D's office. Memo was D's Took memo from billfold	No Robbery
	Carrying Away	Ø	
	Personal Property of Another	Ø	
	Force or Fear	Ø	
	Intent to Deprive	Ø	
HOMICIDE	Killing of Another	D killed B with lance	Homicide
	Causation Actual	"But for" Lance thrown by D	
	Proximate	Death from lance foreseeable	
MURDER	Killing of Another	Supra	Murder
	Malice Specific Intent to Kill Specific Intent to Cause Serious Harm Willful, Wanton Conduct	Saw B slashing paintings Threw lance as B slashed " " " " " "	
FIRST DEGREE MURDER	Specific Intent to Kill	Ran into museum and saw B slashing Threw lance	No First Degree Murder
	Premeditation/Deliberation	Ø	
SECOND DEGREE MURDER	All Murder Not First Degree	Supra	Second Degree Murder
JUSTIFICATION-CRIME PREVENTION	Deadly Force	Threw lance at B	No Defense
	Dangerous Felony	Broke and entered museum Nighttime Slashing painting Burglary museum Mitigation?	
DEFENSE OF PROPERTY	Deadly Force	Threw lance	No Defense
	Protect Home	Guard resided in museum Protecting rare painting loaned (Mitigation?)	

(I)	(R)	(A)	(C)
VOLUNTARY MANSLAUGHTER	Murder	Supra	Voluntary Manslaughter
	Mitigation-Provocation		
	Heat of Passion	Bleeding unconscious guard Museum door broken open Grabbed lance from exhibit B slashing rare paintings Too stunned to react (heat of passion) Threw lance Quickly recovered (cooling off)	
	Mitigation-Imperfect Defenses	Supra	

EXAMPLE OF IRAC CRIMINAL LAW ISSUE

(I) **Robbery Of The Billfold**

(R) Robbery is (1) the trespassory taking and (2) carrying away of (3) the personal property of another through (4) force or fear, with (5) the specific intent to permanently deprive.

(A) When Dave "slipped Amos' billfold from his pocket and ran off with it without consent," such conduct suffices for (1) a trespassory taking and (2) carrying away of (3) Amos' personal property.

Further Dave's act of sticking a pipe in Amos' back frightened Amos into believing that his life was in danger. The fact that Amos raised his hands when told to do so "or I'll shoot" demonstrated that he (4) feared for his life.

Dave will rebut that Amos was never in danger since the pipe was not a deadly weapon. Therefore, his fear was unreasonable.

However, Amos had no way of knowing that the pipe was not a gun. Under such circumstances, his subjective fear was reasonable.

In addition, when Dave threw Amos' billfold under the street light, knowing that a passerby could undoubtedly pick it up, his reckless conduct would equate to (5) a specific intent to permanently deprive Amos of his wallet.

Dave will counter that he threw it under the street light where he "expected Amos to find it." Therefore, he never intended to permanently deprive Amos of his wallet.

Yet, Dave's abandonment of the billfold on a lighted street created a substantial risk of loss. The likelihood of Amos finding it was slim. Therefore, the risk of loss would equate to permanent deprivation.

(C) Dave should be charged with the robbery of the billfold.

SUGGESTED MODEL ANSWER

STATE v. DAVE

Robbery of the Billfold

Robbery is the trespassory taking and carrying away of the personal property of another through force or fear, with the specific intent to permanently deprive.

When Dave "slipped Amos' billfold from his pocket and ran off with it without consent," such conduct suffices for a trespassory taking and carrying away of Amos' personal property.

Further Dave's act of sticking a pipe in Amos' back frightened Amos into believing that his life was in danger. The fact that Amos raised his hands when told to do so "or I'll shoot" demonstrated that he feared for his life.

Dave will rebut that Amos was never in danger since the pipe was not a deadly weapon. Therefore, his fear was unreasonable.

However, Amos had no way of knowing that the pipe was not a gun. Under such circumstances, his subjective fear was reasonable.

Moreover, when Dave threw Amos' billfold under the street light, knowing that a passerby could undoubtedly pick it up, his reckless conduct would equate to a specific intent to permanently deprive Amos of his wallet.

Dave will counter that he threw it under the street light where he "expected Amos to find it." Therefore, he never intended to permanently deprive Amos of his wallet.

Yet, Dave's abandonment of the billfold on a lighted street created a substantial risk of loss. The likelihood of Amos finding it was slim. Therefore, the risk of loss would equate to permanent deprivation.

Dave should be charged with the robbery of the billfold.

Robbery of the Memo

Robbery defined supra.

The State will assert that when Dave took the memo from Amos' billfold without consent, his act was a trespassory taking and carrying away of Amos' personal property.

Dave will counter that the memo belonged to him. Amos had wrongfully gained possession of the memo from Dave's office and was not in rightful possession of it.

Therefore, since Dave was merely recapturing his own property, there was no trespassory taking of the personal property of another.

Dave should not be charged with the robbery of the memo.

Homicide of Bob

Homicide is the killing of one human being by another human being.

Dave's act of throwing the lance at Bob resulted in Bob's death. Thus, a killing occurred.

Actual Causation

"But for" Bob being struck with a lance thrown by Dave, he would not have died. Since Dave put the instrumentality in motion that killed Bob, Dave was the actual cause of Bob's death.

Proximate Causation

When Dave threw the lance at Bob, it directly caused his death. Since it was foreseeable that a death could result, Dave was the proximate cause of Bob's death.

Therefore, a homicide occurred.

Murder

Murder is an unlawful killing of another with malice aforethought.

A killing has been established supra. Dave's conduct demonstrated wanton disregard for Bob's life since the likelihood of death was certain if he was struck. Furthermore, because Dave chose to use a deadly lance, he intended to cause serious bodily injury in his effort to stop Bob's slashing. This manendangering state of mind would equate to malice aforethought.

Thus, Dave committed murder.

First Degree Murder

First degree murder is one committed with the specific intent to kill plus premeditation and deliberation.

When Dave ran into the museum to see Bob slashing his paintings, he threw the lance. However, his intent was to merely cause serious bodily harm as discussed supra. The State would be unable to prove specific intent to kill and it would have to proceed under the theory of murder in the second degree.

Second Degree Murder

Second degree murder is all murder that is not murder in the first degree.

Dave should be charged with murder in the second degree for Bob's death for reasons discussed supra.

Justification - Crime Prevention

Deadly force may be used to prevent the commission of a dangerous felony.

When Dave threw the lance at Bob, he used deadly force. Bob had broken into and entered the Museum at nighttime with the intent to slash the valuable paintings therein. Bob was, thus, engaged in the commission of a dangerous felony, i.e., burglary.

Therefore, Dave will argue that it was necessary for him to use such deadly force in order to prevent the commission of the burglary.

State will counter that the burglary of a museum, although a felony at modern law, would not be considered a dangerous felony sufficient to permit Dave to kill Bob.

Dave could have either called the police or ordered Bob to stop the slashing instead of killing him. Dave's use of deadly force to protect personal property was unreasonable and unjustified.

The State's argument will prevail. However, this imperfect defense may mitigate the murder to voluntary manslaughter (infra).

Defense of Property

One may use deadly force to protect one's dwelling.

Dave will contend that he threw the lance at Bob to protect the museum where the guard resided and worked. Therefore, his use of deadly force to protect the guard's castle was justified.

Further, he was attempting to protect the rare painting that he had loaned to the museum from total destruction. He used the force necessary to accomplish this objective.

However, the "castle" was not Dave's dwelling but was, instead, the guard's. Therefore, his use of deadly force was excessive. Furthermore, deadly force is never justified to protect personal property. Thus, Dave's conduct was unreasonable and unjustified.

The State's argument will prevail although this imperfect defense may mitigate the murder to voluntary manslaughter (infra).

Voluntary Manslaughter

Voluntary manslaughter is a killing that would otherwise be murder but for some legally recognized form of mitigation.

Adequate Provocation

The facts indicate that when Dave saw the bleeding unconscious guard lying by the broken door, he became frightened and grabbed the lance from an exhibit. When he saw Bob slashing at his rare paintings, he reasonably became enraged by Bob's conduct and was provoked to kill him. He was too stunned to react and was unable to think clearly. Due to his "heat of passion", he threw the lance at Bob.

However, even though Dave might have been "stunned" by what he saw, the fact that he "quickly recovered" and then threw the lance demonstrates that he had sufficient time to "cool off" before killing Bob.

Dave will rebut that the time interval between the provocation and the killing would not have given a reasonable person time to regain his senses. Therefore, although Bob's conduct was not sufficient to provoke Dave's use of deadly force, it may be sufficient to mitigate the charge from murder to voluntary manslaughter.

Imperfect Defenses - Crime Prevention/Defense of Property

In addition, Dave will argue that even though his use of deadly force was not justified as discussed supra, the court may recognize these imperfect defenses as a form of mitigation.

Dave should be charged with voluntary manslaughter.

CRIMINAL LAW QUESTION #3

STATE v. DON/OSCAR

Don, in need of funds, approached Oscar, a friend, who sold stereo equipment. Oscar told Don that he had no ready cash to give him, but owned thousands of dollars worth of readily saleable and fully insured stereo equipment stored in a nearby warehouse that he also owned. Don replied that if this were the case Oscar would not lose any money if some of the equipment "disappeared", and Don sold it. Oscar then said he would give Don a duplicate key to the warehouse so that Don, with Don's brother Allen, could remove the equipment, on condition that Don reimburse him for any loss for which he could not recover from his insurance company. Don said, "that's great", and left with the key.

Don told Allen about the plan and Allen agreed to help him. Don and Allen entered the warehouse with the key, and the two men loaded Don's truck with $50,000 worth of equipment. After the items were removed and the warehouse locked, it was agreed that Allen would immediately drive the truck and equipment to Mexico, to be joined later by Don. It was also agreed that Don should go home by means of an automobile which the two had observed in an enclosed parking area to the rear of the warehouse.

Allen drove away and Don reentered the warehouse to reach the parking area. He took the automobile and with it rammed through the locked gate of the fence that enclosed the parking area and proceeded to his apartment.

Allen was driving in excess of the speed limit when a highway patrol car attempted to stop him. Allen, believing the theft had been discovered, attempted to escape by driving at over 100 miles per hour. In the ensuing chase the highway patrol officer lost control of the highway patrol car and was killed when his car overturned.

(A) Has Don committed burglary (1) in the removal of the stereo equipment or (2) in the theft of the vehicle? Discuss.

(B) Is Don guilty of either murder or manslaughter in the death of the highway patrol officer? Discuss.

(C) Is Oscar criminally liable for any crime or crimes committed by Don? Discuss.

IRAC OUTLINE SHEET

(I)	(R)	(A)	(C)

EXAMPLE OF PROPER IRAC OUTLINE

STATE v. DON

(I)	(R)	(A)	(C)
(A) (1) BURGLARY OF STEREO EQUIPMENT			
COMMON LAW BURGLARY			No Common Law Burglary
	Trespassory Breaking	Oscar gave Don a duplicate key Don entered warehouse	
	Entering	Don and Allen entered warehouse	
	Dwelling House of Another	Oscar's Warehouse	
	Nighttime	No facts	
	Intent To Commit Felony Therein	Oscar sold stereo equipment Equipment "disappeared" D and A to remove equipment and sell Recover less from insurance co.	
MODERN LAW BURGLARY	Entrance	Oscar gave Don permission to enter (trespassory?)	No Modern Law Burglary
	Structure	Supra	
	Intent To Commit A Crime Therein	Supra	
(2) BURGLARY OF CAR			
COMMON LAW BURGLARY	Trespassory Breaking	After items removed, warehouse locked D reentered warehouse Reach auto in enclosed parking area Took auto Rammed through locked gate (Break-out theory)	No Common Law Burglary
	Entering	Reentered warehouse	
	Dwelling House of Another	Car/warehouse Auto parked enclosed area	
	Nighttime	No facts	
	Intent to Commit a Crime Therein	Agree that D was to go home in auto which was observed in parking area	
MODERN LAW BURGLARY	Entering	Supra	Modern Law Burglary
	Structure	Supra	
	Intent to Commit a Crime Therein	Supra	
(B) MURDER/MANSLAUGHTER OF CHP OFFICER			
CONSPIRACY	Agreement	D told A about the plan (supra) A agreed to help. Also agreed D go home by auto	
	Two Or More Persons	Don/Allen	Conspiracy
	Specific Intent/Unlawful Act	Defraud insurance company (supra) Home by auto in rear of warehouse	
PINKERTON'S RULE	Acts Within foreseeable Scope Of Conspiracy	After removed, agreed A would immediately drive truck/ equipment to Mexico to be joined later by D A driving in excess of speed?	Arguable
HOMICIDE	Killing of Another	CHP officer was killed while chasing A	Arguable
	Causation Actual	Allen driving 100mph CHP lost control of car (but for)	
	Proximate	Death foreseeable?	

(I)	(R)	(A)	(C)
MURDER	Killing of Another	Supra	
	Malice Felony Murder	 Burglary of vehicle (supra) A driving truck in excess of speed limit CHP attempted to stop A A believed theft discovered. Attempted to escape, officer killed (Casual link to felony?)	No Felony Murder
	Wanton Conduct	100 mph on highway	Arguable
FIRST DEGREE MURDER	Specific Intent To Kill	Driving 100 mph	No First Degree Murder
	Premeditation/Deliberation	Driving 100mph	
SECOND DEGREE MURDER	All Murder Not First Degree	Driving 100 mph	Second Degree Murder
INVOLUNTARY MANSLAUGHTER	Unintentional Killing Without Malice (Criminal Negligence)	100mph on highway Traveling in excess of speed limit	?

(C) **STATE v. OSCAR**

LIABILITY FOR CRIMES OF DON

(I)	(R)	(A)	(C)
CONSPIRACY	Agreement	Don and Oscar agreed to defraud insurance co (supra)	Conspiracy
	Two Or More Persons	Don and Oscar needed funds	
	Specific Intent/Unlawful Act	Defraud insurance co	
PINKERTON'S RULE	Acts Within Foreseeable Scope of Conspiracy	Defraud insurance co (supra) Burglary of auto (supra)? Killing of officer (supra)?	

EXAMPLE OF IRAC CRIMINAL LAW ISSUE

(I) **Common Law Burglary**

(R) Common law burglary is (1) the trespassory breaking and (2) entering of (3) the dwelling house of another in (4) the nighttime with (5) the specific intent to commit a felony therein.

(A) Don will argue that when Oscar, the owner of the warehouse, gave him a duplicate key so that he could enter it, his use of the key to gain access was with the owner's consent. Thus, (1) no trespassory breaking and (2) entering existed.

Further, the warehouse was used for storing stereo equipment. It was not (3) the dwelling place of another. The facts do not indicate that the entry was made in (4) the nighttime as required.

The State will assert that Oscar and Don intended to remove the stereo equipment that Oscar normally sold, make it look like it "disappeared," sell it and then recover the "losses" from the insurance company. This conduct demonstrated Don's (5) specific intent to defraud the insurance company which would constitute a felony therein.

(C) However, due to the lack of a trespassory breaking, dwelling house and nighttime the State will not be able to prove common law burglary of the stereo equipment.

SUGGESTED MODEL ANSWER

STATE v. DON

(A) (1) Burglary of Stereo Equipment

Common Law Burglary

Common law burglary is the trespassory breaking and entering of the dwelling house of another in the nighttime with the specific intent to commit a felony therein.

Don will argue that when Oscar, the owner of the warehouse, gave him a duplicate key so that he could enter it, his use of the key to gain access was with the owner's consent. Thus, no trespassory breaking and entering existed.

Further, the warehouse was used for storing stereo equipment. It was not the dwelling place of another. The facts do not indicate that the entry was mad in the nighttime as required.

The State will assert that Oscar and Don intended to remove the stereo equipment that Oscar normally sold, make it look like it "disappeared," sell it and then recover the "losses" from the insurance company. This conduct demonstrated Don's specific intent to defraud the insurance company which would constitute a felony therein.

However, due to the lack of a trespassory breaking, dwelling house and nighttime the State will not be able to prove common law burglary of the stereo equipment.

Modern Law Burglary of Stereo Equipment

Modernly, a burglary is the entrance into a structure with the intent to commit a crime therein.

As discussed supra, since Don entered the warehouse with a duplicate key pursuant to Oscar's consent, there was an entrance. A split of jurisdictions exists as to whether or not an entrance must be unlawful/trespassory at modern law. The majority of jurisdictions have required the entrance to be unlawful which has not been satisfied in this instance. Even though the warehouse would suffice as a structure and intent to commit a crime was present, there is no modern law burglary of the stereo equipment in a majority of jurisdictions.

(2) Burglary of Car

Common Law Burglary

As defined supra.

The State will argue that the key to the warehouse was given to Don for the purpose of allowing him entry to take the stereo equipment. When Don locked the warehouse after the items were removed and then reentered to gain access to the car in the enclosed parking area, Don exceeded Oscar's consent. The reentry was, therefore, a trespassory breaking and entering.

When Don gained access to the car without consent, he committed a further trespassory breaking and entering. In addition, when Don rammed the stolen car through the locked gate of the fence that enclosed the parking area, he committed a breaking under the common law break-out theory.

However, neither the warehouse nor the car constitutes a dwelling house of another. There are no facts to indicate the taking of the car occurred in the nighttime. Even though it was agreed that Don was to go home in the auto that had been observed in the parking area demonstrating his specific intent to commit a theft of the car, it appears that no common law burglary was committed.

Modern Law Burglary

As defined supra.

As set forth supra, the State will contend that when Don reentered the warehouse, he exceeded the previous consent of Oscar. Thus, his entry was trespassory.

Furthermore, the warehouse or the car will suffice as a structure under the modern law.

Finally, Don intended to steal the car when he reentered the warehouse. Thus, he had the specific intent to commit a crime therein (supra).

It appears that Don committed modern law burglary.

(B) Murder/Manslaughter of Highway Patrol Officer

Conspiracy

A conspiracy is an agreement between two or more person with the specific intent to commit an unlawful act.

Don told Allen about the plan to defraud the insurance company and Allen agreed to help him. They agreed that Don should go home by means of an automobile in the warehouse parking area, thus, establishing the requisite agreement between two persons.

Since Allen was aware of the "plan," he specifically intended to commit the unlawful acts of attempting to defraud the insurance company and stealing a car.

Therefore Don and Allen are guilty of conspiracy.

Pinkerton's Rule

Each member of a conspiracy is chargeable with all crimes in furtherance of or the natural and probable consequence of the unlawful act.

The State will assert that the original agreement between Don and Allen was that "Allen would immediately drive the truck and equipment to Mexico to be joined later by Don." Allen's act of driving to Mexico in excess of the speed limit in order to execute the plan was foreseeably within the scope of the original conspiracy.

Don will counter that acts of alleged burglary and insurance fraud were completed when the stereo equipment had been removed from the warehouse and the car had been removed from the parking area. Therefore, the res gestae of the crimes had been completed, making Allen's subsequent act of speeding outside the scope of the conspiracy.

However, it would appear that Allen's act of speeding to Mexico would be deemed a foreseeable and reasonable response in light of the immediacy of the situation.

Therefore, liability would extend to Don for any acts that Allen committed while completing the crime.

Homicide

Homicide is the killing of one human being by another human being.

The State will argue that since the highway patrol officer died when he lost control of his car while pursuing Allen at high speed, there was a killing of a human being by another.

Actual Causation

"But for" Allen's conduct of trying to escape at 100 miles per hour, the highway patrol officer would not have given chase. He would not have lost control of his car to be killed when it overturned. Therefore, Allen was the actual cause of the officer's death.

Proximate Causation

Allen created a risk to the officer by driving at 100 miles per hour. It was foreseeable that the officer would institute an ensuing chase of a speeding automobile. Even though the overturning of the officer's car could be seen as an intervening act, it was the natural and foreseeable consequence of Allen's actions. Allen's conduct was the proximate cause of the officer's death.

Therefore, the officer's death was a homicide.

Murder

Murder is an unlawful killing of another with malice aforethought.

A killing has been established supra. The State will argue that the death of the officer was committed during the burglary of the automobile supra. Since burglary is considered an inherently dangerous felony, there has been a felony murder which constitutes malice.

However, the burglary of the car at the warehouse was not causally related to the death of the officer. The officer attempted to stop Allen because of his truck's excessive speed. The chase of Allen's speeding truck had nothing to do with the discovery of the burglary in the theft of the auto. The officer's death was not within the res geste of the felony. Therefore, no felony murder existed.

In the alternative, the State will argue wanton conduct in that Allen was driving over 100 miles per hour. This conduct would have given him the knowledge that he was creating a serious risk of harm to the highway patrol officer as well as others.

Therefore, Allen acted with the necessary wanton and reckless conduct to establish malice.

The death of the highway patrol officer was murder.

First Degree Murder

First degree murder is one committed with the specific intent to kill plus premeditation and deliberation.

Since Allen's act of driving 100 miles per hour alone does not indicate a specific intent to kill plus premeditation and deliberation, this will not be a first degree murder.

Second Degree Murder

Second degree murder is all murder which is not murder in the first degree.

Based on the foregoing, it would appear that the death of the officer was murder in the second degree.

Involuntary Manslaughter

Involuntary manslaughter is an unintentional killing without malice.

If it is found that Allen's conduct was not sufficiently wanton, the State will argue that by traveling on the highway at speeds of more than 100 miles per hour, Allen was acting in disregard to the lives of other motorists including the of the officer. Such reckless conduct would be sufficient at a minimum to constitute criminal negligence.

Therefore, absent a finding of malice for murder, Allen should be found guilty of involuntary manslaughter which will be imputed to Don under accomplice liability (supra).

STATE v. OSCAR

(C) Conspiracy

As defined supra.

Oscar agreed to supply Don with a duplicate key to the warehouse. When Don promised to reimburse Oscar for any losses that were not covered by his insurance, the two formed an agreement between two or more persons with the specific intent to commit the unlawful act of insurance fraud.

Therefore, a conspiracy was formed.

Pinkerton's Rule

As defined supra.

Oscar will contend that he is liable only for those acts which were necessary and foreseeable in order to carry out his agreement with Don.

Don and Allen had finished taking the stereo equipment from the warehouse and had locked the warehouse before they decided to steal the car in the parking area. Therefore, Don and Allen's act of stealing the car was unrelated to Oscar's agreement with Don.

Further, when the officer began chasing Allen, he was doing so because of Allen's excessive speed. The chase of the truck was unrelated to the agreement to defraud the insurance company. Speeding to Mexico was neither necessary nor foreseeable under the circumstances. Therefore, these acts were outside the scope of the agreement.

Oscar should not be prosecuted for the burglary of the auto or the murder/manslaughter of the officer.

CRIMINAL LAW QUESTION #4

STATE v. BOB/JIM

Bob, age 13, and Hal, age 16, bored by the prospect of another long summer afternoon, set out on their favorite pastime -- rummaging through the garages and toolsheds of neighbors. In the past they had sometimes merely used but had sometimes taken tools kept there. Hal's young brother Jim, age 6, tagged along for the first time.

The boys entered Smith's garage, which was attached to the rear of the home, through the closed but unlocked garage door. Bob and Hal rummaged through the tool boxes and practiced cutting wood on the table saw. Jim, alone near a corner shelf in the garage, saw a gold watch which had been left there inadvertently by Smith. Jim picked up the watch, put it in his pocket, and without a word left for home.

After about a hour in the garage Bob and Hal also left and continued to Jones' toolshed for the stated purpose of taking a large screwdriver which had, on a prior occasion, caught Bob's fancy. Jones' shed was detached and about 50 yards from his house. Although the door was always locked, the boys had never had difficulty in prying open the door and on this occasion they again broke the lock. As Hal pushed the door open and stepped into the shed he was shot in the head, suffering a fatal wound.

On the prior evening Jones had mounted a loaded pistol in the shed, aimed at the door and connected so that the pistol would discharge if the door was pushed open. Jones told the police he mounted the gun to protect his property from thieves, that he intended to scare them away and did not intend to kill anyone. No statute prohibited the use of spring guns.

1. Bob and Jim are charged with burglary of Smiths' garage and larceny of Smith's watch.

2. Bob is charged with burglary of Jones' toolshed.

3. Jones is charged with murder of Hal.

What result as to each charge? Discuss.

IRAC OUTLINE SHEET

(I)	(R)	(A)	(C)

EXAMPLE OF PROPER IRAC OUTLINE

STATE v. BOB (B)/JIM (J):

(I)	(R)	(A)	(C)
(1.A) C/L BURGLARY OF GARAGE	Trespassory Breaking	Boys entered through closed/unlocked garage door	No Burglary
	Entering	Boys entered	
	Dwelling House of Another	Garage/attached to rear of home	
	Nighttime	Long summer afternoon	
	Intent to Commit Felony Therein	Favorite pastime/rummaging sometimes use/sometimes taken tools	
M/L BURGLARY OF GARAGE	Entrance	Supra	No Burglary
	Structure	Garage	
	Intent To Commit a Crime Therein	Supra	
(B) LARCENY OF WATCH (JIM)	Trespassory Taking	J picked up Smith's watch/put in pocket	Larceny
	Carrying Away	Left for home	
	Personal Property of Another	Smith's watch Watch inadvertently left by Smith	
	Specific Intent Deprive	Without a word/left for home	
EXCUSE—INFANCY	Age 0-6 Conclusive Presumption	J age 6	Valid Excuse
CONSPIRACY (BOB)	Agreement	J tagged along for first time Favorite pastime (Supra)	No Conspiracy
	Two or More Persons	J	
	Specific Intent/Unlawful Act	J alone near corner shelf/saw watch Without a word (Supra)	

STATE v. BOB (B)

(I)	(R)	(A)	(C)
2. C/L BURGLARY OF TOOLSHED	Trespassory Breaking	Jones' tooted/door always locked Boys broke lock	No Burglary
	Entering	Hal pushed door open/stepped into shed	
	Dwelling House of Another	Shed detached/50 yards from house	
	Nighttime	Bored with prospect long summer afternoon/about hour in garage went to shed	
	Intent to Commit A Crime	Continued to Jones' toolshed/stated purpose of taking large screwdriver/ on prior occasion, caught B's fancy	
M/L BURGLARY OF TOOLSHED	Entrance	Supra	Arguable
	Structure	Toolshed	
	Intent To Commit A Crime	Supra	
EXCUSE-INFANCY	Age 7-13 Rebuttable Presumption	B age 13	Arguable

(I)	(R)	(A)	(C)
<u>STATE v. JONES</u>			
3. HOMICIDE OF HAL (H)	Killing of Another	H suffered fatal head wound	Homicide
	Causation		
	Actual	Mounted loaded pistol/aimed at door/connected to discharge if door pushed open (But for?)	
	Proximate	Mounted loaded pistol (Supra) (Foreseeable?)	
MURDER	Killing of Another	Supra	Murder
	Malice		
	Specific Intent/To Kill	Mounted loaded gun (supra)	
	Specific Intent To Cause Bodily Harm	Aimed at door Intended to scare	
	Wanton Conduct	See malice facts above	
	Felony Murder	No Statute prohibited	
FIRST DEGREE MURDER	Specific Intent to Kill	Mounted to protect/intended to scare/not kill	No First Degree Murder
	Premeditation/Deliberation	Aimed at door/connected to discharge	
SECOND DEGREE MURDER	All Murder Not First Degree	See 1st degree murder facts	Second Degree Murder
JUSTIFICATION-DEFENSE OF PROPERTY	Deadly Force	Mounted gun	No Defense
	Protect Home	Tool shed 50 yards from home/	
JUSTIFICATION-CRIME PREVENTION	Deadly Force	Mounted gun	
	Dangerous Felony	Taking of a screwdriver	
VOLUNTARY MANSLAUGHTER	Murder	Supra	
	Mitigation-Imperfect Defenses	See facts under justification	Voluntary Manslaughter

EXAMPLE OF IRAC CRIMINAL LAW ISSUE

(I) **Larceny Of Smith's Watch (Jim)**

(R) Larceny is (1) the trespassory taking and (2) carrying away of (3) the personal property of another with (4) the specific intent to permanently deprive.

(A) When Jim picked up Smith's watch and put it in his pocket without consent, his conduct was (1) a trespassory taking. His act of leaving for home with it was sufficient asportation to prove (2) a carrying away.

Since the watch had been inadvertently left by Smith, he did not intend to abandon it. As such, Smith retained constructive possession and the watch would remain Smith's (3) personal property.

The fact that Jim left for home with the watch in his pocket without a word to the other boys indicates that at the time of taking, he intended to keep the watch for himself. This would equate to (4) the specific intent to permanently deprive Smith of his watch.

(C) Jim has committed a larceny.

SUGGESTED MODEL ANSWER

STATE v. BOB/JIM

1.(a) Common Law Burglary Of Smith's Garage

Common law burglary is the trespassory breaking and entering of the dwelling house of another in the nighttime with the specific intent to commit a felony therein.

When Bob and Jim arrived at Smith's garage, the door was closed but unlocked. Bob's act of opening the door to create a passageway where none previously existed, without Smith's consent, constituted a trespassory breaking. The boys entered the garage. Since the garage was not used for purpose of sleeping, it would not generally suffice as a dwelling of another. However, because it was physically attached to the rear of Smith's home, it would be close enough to the residence to be included within reasonable fencing. As such, it would fall within the curtilege of the dwelling of another.

The facts indicate that the boys were bored with the prospect of another long summer afternoon. If their activities took place during that time of day, the requirement of nighttime would not be satisfied.

Further, Bob and Jim merely set out on their favorite pastime -- rummaging through the garages and toolsheds of their neighbors. Even though they sometimes used and sometimes took tools, there are insufficient facts to prove a specific intent to commit a felony in Smith's garage on this occasion.

Therefore, Bob and Jim will not be convicted of common law burglary.

Modern Law Burglary

Modernly, a burglary is the entrance into a structure with the intent to commit a crime therein.

As discussed supra, an entrance has been satisfied. There is a split of jurisdiction as to whether that entrance must be trespassory. In either jurisdiction, there will be no problem proving this element as discussed supra.

The garage will suffice as a structure. However, as previously discussed, the element of intent is lacking.

Bob and Jim cannot be convicted of modern law burglary.

(b) Larceny of Smith's Watch (Jim)

Larceny is the trespassory taking and carrying away of the personal property of another with the specific intent to permanently deprive.

When Jim picked up Smith's watch and put it in his pocket without consent, his conduct was a trespassory taking. His act of leaving for home with it was sufficient asportation to prove a carrying away.

Since the watch had been inadvertently left by Smith, he did not intend to abandon it. As such, Smith retained constructive possession and the watch would remain Smith's personal property.

The fact that Jim left for home with the watch in his pocket without a word to the other boys indicates that at the time of taking, he intended to keep the watch would for himself. This would equate to the specific intent to permanently deprive Smith of his watch.

Jim has committed a larceny.

Excuse/Infancy

Common law conclusively presumes that a child under the age of seven is incapable of forming criminal intent and, thus, cannot be convicted of a crime.

Since Jim was six years of age, under common law, he would be incapable of forming the specific intent necessary to prove a larceny (supra).

Therefore, Jim will not be criminally responsible for the larceny.

Conspiracy To Commit Larceny (Bob)

A conspiracy is an agreement between two or more persons with the specific intent to commit an unlawful act.

Jim tagged along with Bob and Hal for the first time when they went to Smith's garage to engage in their favorite pastime of rummaging. When Jim saw the watch, he was alone near a corner shelf. He took the watch without a word to Bob or Hal. As such, no agreement, tacit or express, was formed between two or more persons to commit the unlawful act of larceny.

Bob cannot be convicted of larceny through an underlying conspiracy.

STATE v. BOB

2. Common Law Burglary of Jones' Toolshed

Defined supra.

When Bob and Hal broke the lock on Jones' toolshed in order to gain entrance where no previous opening existed, they did so without consent sufficient to prove a trespassory breaking.

It was Hal who pushed the door open and stepped into the shed. There are no facts to show an entrance by Bob.

However, State may counter that Hal and Bob were acting in concert. Thus, Hal's entrance equated to an entry by Bob.

Further, the shed was detached from the Jones' home and located 50 yards from it. As such, the toolshed would not be within the curtilege of the home and could not be considered the dwelling house of another.

Finally, the boys' activities at Jones' toolshed appear to have taken place within an hour of their similar acts at Smith's garage. If so, it would still have been afternoon which is insufficient to satisfy the common law requirement for nighttime.

Even though Bob proceeded to Jones' toolshed for the stated purpose of taking a large screwdriver that had caught his fancy on a prior occasion, demonstrating his specific intent to commit a crime therein, he cannot be convicted of common law burglary.

Modern Law Burglary

Defined supra.

As discussed supra, the state may have difficulty proving an entrance by Bob. The toolshed will suffice as a structure and specific intent has been shown supra.

Thus, Bob will probably not be convicted of modern law burglary.

Excuse/Infancy

At common law, a child between seven and fourteen years of age is rebuttably presumed incapable of forming criminal intent.

If Bob is convicted of modern law burglary supra, he will argue that he was thirteen years old. As such, he may de presumed incapable if forming the specific intent necessary for burglary. However, since he had seen the screwdriver on previous occasions and went back for the express purpose to taking it, he arguably knew hat he was doing, and that it was wrong.

Thus, the presumption may be rebutted and infancy will not excuse the crime.

STATE v. JONES

3. Homicide of Hal

Homicide in the killing of one human being by another human being.

Hal suffered a fatal head wound from a gun mounted by Jones. Thus, a killing occurred.

Actual Causation

"But for" Jones' act of mounting a loaded pistol aimed at the shed door which was connected to the discharge when the door was pushed open, Hal would not have been killed. Jones was the actual cause of Hal's killing.

Proximate Causation

It was foreseeable that when a loaded pistol was mounted and aimed at head level and connected to discharge when the door was opened, a death would result. Jones was the proximate cause of Hal's death.

A homicide occurred.

Murder

Murder is an unlawful killing of another with malice aforethought.

A killing has been established supra. Although Jones stated to the police that he did not intend for the mounted gun to kill, the fact that he used such a dangerous instrumentality to scare thieves, may show an intent to cause serious bodily harm. At a minimum, his conduct demonstrates a reckless disregard for human life. A non-deadly instrumentality could have achieved the same goal without the potential for death. This is sufficient willful and wanton conduct to establish malice.

Since there was no statute that prohibited the use of such instrumentalities in that jurisdiction, the State will not be able to prove malice through the additional manendangering state of mind of felony murder.

Therefore, Jones may be convicted of murder.

First Degree Murder

First Degree murder is one committed with the specific intent to kill plus premeditation and deliberation.

The State will have difficulty proving a specific intent to kill as discussed supra. Even though Jones' act of mounting the gun and aiming could be sufficient to prove a calculated and planned act i.e., premeditation and deliberation, Jones may not be convicted of first degree murder.

Second Degree Murder

Second degree murder is all murder that is not murder in the first degree.

Since murder has been proven, Jones may be convicted of second degree murder.

Justification - Defense of Property

One may use deadly force to protect one's dwelling.

Jones' use of a deadly mounted gun exceeded the force permitted to protect his toolshed from Hal's unlawful intrusion, because the toolshed was not Jones' dwelling. Since the law does not justify the sacrifice of a life in order to secure property from non-deadly intrusions, Jones will not prevail under this defense.

Justification - Crime Prevention

Deadly force may be used to prevent the commission of a dangerous felony.

Jones' used of a mounted gun was deadly force. However, it was used to prevent the taking of a screwdriver which was not suffice as a dangerous felony, but rather a petit larceny.

Therefore, Jones will not prevail under crime prevention.

Voluntary Manslaughter - Imperfect Defenses

Voluntary manslaughter is a killing that would otherwise be murder but for some legally recognized from of mitigation.

Jones will argue that even though his defenses discussed supra may not entirely justify his crime under the circumstances, such would suffice as imperfect defenses which would mitigate his crime to voluntary manslaughter.

Jones should be convicted of voluntary manslaughter.

CRIMINAL LAW QUESTION #5

STATE v. DONALD

Donald has been separated from his wife, Veronica, for over a year, but they are still legally married. He had recently made overtures to her about getting back together again, but she had rebuffed him, claiming she was interested in "going it alone."

On the evening in question, Donald learned from a friend of Veronica that she was not in fact "going it alone" but was involved with another man. Donald went over to Veronica's house, carrying a crowbar. He intended to enter house and force her to have sexual relations with him, using the crowbar if she physically resisted. Donald was completely unaware that, in the jurisdiction in which he and Veronica live, it is not a crime for a husband forcibly to require his wife to submit to sex with him, regardless of whether the spouses are co-habitants.

Donald entered the downstairs level of the house close to midnight. Veronica was awakened from a deep sleep by noise made by Donald and, when she looked into the downstairs hallway, she saw what appeared to her to be the shadowy figure of a man with a crowbar. She escaped from the house by climbing out of a second story window and as she was shimmying down a nearby tree, she fell off a branch, dying instantly when she hit the ground.

Based on the foregoing facts, is there sufficient evidence to convict Donald of:

1. Burglary, under a statute that states in relevant part, "Every person who enters a home with intent to commit a crime therein is guilty of burglary?" Discuss.

2. First degree murder under the felony-murder rule? Discuss.

IRAC OUTLINE SHEET

(I)	(R)	(A)	(C)

EXAMPLE OF PROPER IRAC OUTLINE

STATE v. DONALD

(I)	(R)	(A)	(C)
STATUTORY BURGLARY	Entrance	D separated from wife, V over a year V rebuffed D's recent overtures to get back together/V claimed "go it alone" D entered the downstairs level of the house close to midnight	Statutory Burglary
	Home	V's house	
	Intent Crime Therein	D learned from friend V "not going it alone/involved with other man D intended to enter house/force sex using crowbar if V physically resisted D unaware that it was not a crime for husband to force sex on wife whether co-habitant or not-(Mistake of Law)	
HOMICIDE	Killing of Another	V escaped for house out window/ shimmied down tree/fell from branch/died instantly when hit the ground	Homicide
	Causation		
	Actual	But for V's seeing shadowy figure with crowbar in hallway/escaped out window/ fell/died	
	Proximate	V was awakened from a deep sleep by noises made by D V saw shadowy figure with crowbar/ escaped out second story window/shimmied down tree/fell off branch/died instantly (foreseeable?)	
MURDER	Killing of Another	Supra	Murder
	Malice	D went to V's house carrying a crowbar	
	Specific Intent to Cause Serious Bodily Harm	D intended to force sex/use crowbar if V resisted	
	Willful/Wanton Conduct	Force sex/use crowbar	
	Felony Murder	Statutory Burglary supra	
FIRST DEGREE MURDER	Specific Intent to kill	Intended to use crowbar to force sexual relations if V resisted	First Degree Murder
	Premeditation/Deliberation	D went to house supra	
	Felony Murder	Statutory Burglary supra	

EXAMPLE OF IRAC CRIMINAL LAW ISSUE

(I) **Statutory Burglary**

(R) Every person who (1) enters (2) a home (3) with intent to commit a crime therein is guilty of burglary.

(A) Donald has been separated from Veronica for over a year at the time that he (1) entered the downstairs level of her (2) house. Since Veronica had rebuffed his recent overtures to get back together claiming that she wanted to "go it alone," it can be assumed that his midnight entrance was without consent making it trespassory in nature.

Further, (3) Donald intended to force Veronica to have sexual relations with him which the State will argue is a crime therein.

Donald will counter that even though he intended to force sexual relations on Veronica, she was his wife. Despite the fact that they did not co-habitate, force sexual relations by a husband on a wife was not a crime in the jurisdiction where he was being prosecuted. His lack of awareness of this at the time of his advances would not change the fact that his intended activity was not a crime under the governing law.

Therefore, mistake of law should negate Donald's intent to commit a crime therein.

However, Donald's intent was not only to enter the house to force sexual relations on Veronica. That evening, he had learned from a friend that Veronica was not "going it alone", but was involved with another man. Upon learning this, he took a crowbar with him intending to use it on her if she resisted his advances.

Since Donald clearly carried the crowbar with him to commit the crimes of assault and/or battery, he intended to commit a crime therein.

(C) Donald will be guilty of statutory burglary.

SUGGESTED MODEL ANSWER

STATE v. DONALD

1. Statutory Burglary

Every person who enters a home with intent to commit a crime therein is guilty of burglary.

Donald had been separated from Veronica for over one year at the time that he entered the downstairs level of her house. Since Veronica had rebuffed his recent overtures to get back together claiming that she wanted to "go it alone," it can be assumed that his midnight entrance was without consent, making it trespassory in nature.

Further, Donald intended to force Veronica to have sexual relations with him, which the State will argue is a crime therein.

Donald will counter that even though he intended to force sexual relations on Veronica, she was his wife. Despite the fact that they did not co-habitate, forced sexual relations by a husband on a wife was not a crime in the jurisdiction where he was being prosecuted. His lack of awareness of this at the time of his advances would not change the fact that his intended activity was not a crime under the governing law.

Therefore, mistake of law should negate Donald's intent to commit a crime therein.

However, Donald's intent was not only to enter the house to force sexual relations on Veronica. That evening, he had learned from a friend that Veronica was not "going it alone," but was involved with another man. Upon learning this, he took a crowbar with him intending to use in on her if she resisted his advances.

Since Donald clearly carried the crowbar with him to commit the crimes of assault and/or battery, he intended to commit a crime therein.

Donald will be guilty of statutory burglary.

2. Homicide

Homicide is the killing of one human being by another human being.

Veronica died instantly when she fell from a branch of the tree that she was shimmying down in an effort to flee from Donald. Her death during an escape from a second-story window clearly demonstrates the killing of a human being by another.

Actual Causation

"But for" Veronica's being frightened by Donald's shadowy figure in her hallway with a crowbar, she would not have fallen to her death from the window during her escape.

Thus, Donald was the actual cause of her death.

Proximate Causation

The State will assert that when a lone sleeping woman is awakened from a deep sleep by noises in her house, and sees the shadowy figure of a man with a crowbar, it is foreseeable that she will become frightened and attempt to escape. Since she was in a second story bedroom, it was foreseeable that her flight through the nearest window could result in injuries.

Donald will rebut that it was not foreseeable that Veronica would shimmy down a tree and fall off a tree branch to her death.

However, escape is the natural and probable consequence of a residential burglary. In any form, escape carries with it a foreseeable risk of harm. Even through the sequence of events may not have been foreseeable, the result, i.e., bodily injury including death, was foreseeable. Since it is the foreseeability of result which determines liability, the State has the stronger argument.

Donald is the proximate cause of Veronica's death sufficient to show a homicide.

Murder

Murder is an unlawful killing of another with malice aforethought.

A killing has been established supra. When Donald entered Veronica's house with the intent to use a crowbar to force sexual relations on her if she resisted, he had the specific intent to cause serious bodily harm. A crowbar is an extremely dangerous instrumentality capable of causing death. The very use of it to satisfy his sexual appetite demonstrates his abandoned, malignant heart and his reckless disregard for Veronica's life. This equates to willful, wanton conduct through which malice aforethought can be established.

Further, Veronica was attempting to escape during the res geste of the burglary (supra). Thus, her death was causally connected to the perpetration of the crime. These facts are sufficient for proof of felony murder which equates to malice aforethought.

Donald will be found guilty of murder.

First Degree Murder

First degree murder is one committed with the specific intent to kill plus premeditation and deliberation or felony murder.

The State will argue that when Donald took the crowbar with him to Veronica's house, his use of such a dangerous instrumentality indicates that he intended to kill her. However, since the facts state that his intent was to use it to force sexual relations on her if she physically resisted, it is unlikely that the State will be able to prove specific intent to kill with premeditation and deliberation.

However, as discussed previously under malice, the State will be able to prove felony murder via the burglary which will be sufficient of fine Donald guilty of murder in the first degree.

FLEMING'S FUNDAMENTALS OF LAW

Prices Effective – January 1, 2008

FFOL BAR REVIEW COURSES:

Long Term Live Bar Review Course	$2,900	Short Term Live Bar Review Course	$2,700
Long Term Home Study Bar Review	$3,300	Short Term Home Study Bar Review	$3,100
Ultimate Bar Tutorial	$6,400	Premier Tutorial Package	$6,400

FFOL EXAM SOLUTION® REVIEW COURSES:

With 4 Hour CDs, Outline, Hypotheticals & A Sample Written Model Answer Included For Attached Hypothetical. Audiocassettes also available upon request.

	FFOL Bar Student @ 20% Discount	Non Bar Student		FFOL Bar Student @ 20% Discount	Non Bar Student
Agency / Partnership Outline Only	**$20**	$25	PR for the MPRE Exam	**$68**	$85
Civil Procedure I	**$56**	$70	Property I	**$56**	$70
Civil Procedure II	**$56**	$70	Property II	**$56**	$70
Community Property	**$56**	$70	Remedies	**$68**	$85
Constitutional Law I	**$56**	$70	Torts I	**$56**	$70
Constitutional Law II	**$56**	$70	Torts II	**$56**	$70
Contracts I – U.C.C.	**$56**	$70	Trusts	**$56**	$70
Contracts II – U.C.C.	**$56**	$70	U.C.C. Outline Only	**$20**	$25
Corporations	**$56**	$70	Wills	**$56**	$70
Criminal Law	**$56**	$70			
Criminal Procedure	**$56**	$70	Outlines only for individual subjects listed		
Evidence	**$68**	$85	(excluding PR for MPRE Exam)	**$20**	$25

FFOL COURSES AND SEMINARS:

Legal Examination Writing Workshop			Baby Bar Review		
• Live Program	**$180**	$225	• Live Program	**$380**	$475
• Home Study Program	**$200**	$250	• Home Study Program	**$460**	$575
Performance Review – 4 Days			Final Review Videos		
• Live Program	**$360**	$450	(viewed in Main office)	**$40**	$50
• Home Study Program	**$400**	$500			

FFOL PUBLICATIONS & STUDY AIDS:

Essay Examination Writing Workbook Volume 1 (Torts, Contracts/UCC, Criminal Law)	**$28**	$35	FFOL Multistate Examination Workbook Volume I (Contracts/UCC, Crim. Law, Torts, Prof. Resp., Simulated Exam)	**$28**	$35
Essay Examination Writing Workbook Volume 2 (Evidence, Property, Civil Procedure)	**$28**	$35	FFOL Multistate Examination Workbook Volume II (Civ. Pro., Con. Law, Crim. Pro., Evidence, Property)	**$28**	$35
Essay Examination Writing Workbook Volume 3 (Con Law. Crim. Pro., Corps.)	**$28**	$35	Performance Exam Solution (CD's And Workbook)	**$84**	$105
Essay Examination Writing Workbook Volume 4 (Com. Prop., Wills, Trusts, Remedies)	**$28**	$35	Professional Responsibility Exams & Answers	**$24**	$30

JOIN TODAY

With a $250 non-refundable deposit towards any future FFOL Bar Review, you will receive the following benefits:

- ✓ **Free Exam Solution Outlines®** for the semester in which you join FFOL.
- ✓ A **20% discount** given on all future FFOL courses and materials during law school.
- ✓ Attend all **Final Review Courses free** in your last semester of law school.
- ✓ **Free set of Exam Solution Outlines®** in your last semester of law school.
- ✓ **Your space is reserved** in the bar review and the **course price is frozen.**

Prices DO NOT INCLUDE sales tax, shipping & handling. PRICES ARE SUBJECT TO CHANGE WITHOUT NOTICE.
Visa, Mastercard, American Express, and Discover accepted. No COD's.

26170 Enterprise Way, Suite 500, Lake Forest, CA 92630
1-800-**LAW-EXAM** (CA ONLY) • 949-770-7030 • FAX 949-454-8556
EMAIL: info@ffol.com • WEB: ffol.com